THE REALLY
USEFUL eLEARNING
INSTRUCTION MANUAL

THE REALLY USEFUL eLEARNING INSTRUCTION MANUAL

Your toolkit for putting elearning into practice

Rob Hubbard

WILEY

This edition first published 2013
© 2013 John Wiley & Sons Ltd

Registered office

John Wiley and Sons Ltd, The Atrium, Southern Gate, Chichester, West Sussex, PO19 8SQ, United Kingdom

For details of our global editorial offices, for customer services and for information about how to apply for permission to reuse the copyright material in this book please see our website at www.wiley.com.

Wiley publishes in a variety of print and electronic formats and by print-on-demand. Some material included with standard print versions of this book may not be included in e-books or in print-on-demand. If this book refers to media such as a CD or DVD that is not included in the version you purchased, you may download this material at http://booksupport.wiley.com. For more information about Wiley products, visit www.wiley.com.

Designations used by companies to distinguish their products are often claimed as trademarks. All brand names and product names used in this book and on its cover are trade names, service marks, trademark or registered trademarks of their respective owners. The publisher and the book are not associated with any product or vendor mentioned in this book. None of the companies referenced within the book have endorsed the book.

Limit of Liability/Disclaimer of Warranty: While the publisher and author have used their best efforts in preparing this book, they make no representations or warranties with the respect to the accuracy or completeness of the contents of this book and specifically disclaim any implied warranties of merchantability or fitness for a particular purpose. It is sold on the understanding that the publisher is not engaged in rendering professional services and neither the publisher nor the author shall be liable for damages arising herefrom. If professional advice or other expert assistance is required, the services of a competent professional should be sought.

Library of Congress Cataloging-in-Publication Data

Hubbard, Rob, 1975-
   The really useful elearning instruction manual : your toolkit for putting elearning into practice / Rob Hubbard.
      pages   cm
   Includes index.
   ISBN 978-1-118-37589-1 (pbk.)
      1. Computer-assisted instruction.   2. Educational technology.   I. Title.
   LB1028.5.H78 2013
   371.33'4—dc23

                                                                                    2013027979

A catalogue record for this book is available from the British Library.

ISBN 978-1-118-37589-1 (hardback)   ISBN 978-1-118-37587-7 (ebk)
ISBN 978-1-118-37588-4 (ebk)

Cover design: Andrew Ward

Set in 10/14pt Minion Pro by MPS Limited, Chennai, India
Printed in Great Britain by TJ International Ltd, Padstow, Cornwall, UK

Contents

Preface

It has been my great privilege to be involved in the eLearning Network (eLN) for many years, including four as an elected Board member and two as the Chair. As a Community Interest Company the Board are volunteers and the eLN is owned by its members, existing solely for the good of the elearning community as a whole. The eLN has 3000+ members, judges awards, runs events, provides mentoring, shares knowledge and generally does all it can to enhance the elearning industry.

There were many things I enjoyed about being Chair (the ermine robe, the sceptre, the private jet) but most of all was the opportunity to talk to, work with and generally pick the brains of the smartest people in the elearning industry. So, when Wiley asked me to write this book I immediately thought how much more we could offer with chapters authored by world leading experts in elearning.

Now I might get punched at a conference for saying this – but I don't think you need to know a vast amount of 'stuff' to create effective online learning experiences. You just need to know the 'right stuff' and this typically comes from the 'right people'. So that's what we've done here – assembled the leading experts in each of the main areas of elearning to share their hard-won wisdom, tried and tested methodologies, tips and experience with you.

Knowledge however, is not enough. You need to put it into practice, so we've designed this book to be highly practical. Each chapter follows a set structure and includes hints, tips and guidance to help you explore new areas of elearning whilst avoiding some of the common pitfalls.

This book follows the ethos of the eLN – that of sharing knowledge and helping others for the benefit of all. If having read this book you want more, visit the eLN website http://www.elearningnetwork.org where you'll find further information, support and like-minded people.

Rob Hubbard
Chair of the eLearning Network 2011–2013

1. So What is eLearning?

Clive Shepherd

Clive Shepherd is a consultant learning technologist, writer and speaker. He works with a broad range of public and private sector organizations internationally, helping them to build capability in the application of new media to learning, and to transform workplace learning through the effective integration of formal, informal, on-demand and experiential learning.

He established his interest in interactive media while Director, Training and Creative Services for American Express in EMEA. He went on to co-found Epic, one of the UK's major producers of custom elearning.

He is widely acknowledged as one of the UK's foremost experts in workplace learning and development, with hundreds of published articles to his name. For four years he was Chairman of the eLearning Network. Currently he is a Director of Onlignment Ltd, which provides expertise in all aspects of online communication.

Blog: http://clive-shepherd.blogspot.com
Twitter: cliveshepherd

It might seem strange to start a book on elearning by asking what it is. After all, you've presumably already purchased this book, so you probably have a pretty good idea what it is about. The trouble is, what you call elearning is not necessarily what others mean when they use the same term. Like so much specialist terminology, after a while it becomes ambiguous and confusing, with different camps claiming they have the one true definition. Well, as the author of this first chapter, I have a unique power at my disposal – to squash all this doubt and confusion and settle once and for all what we mean when we say "elearning".

Elearning is when we use computers and the networks to which these are linked to in some way support the learning process.

That's about as broad as I can make it, and it needs to be broad because, in this book, we're going to be adopting a very eclectic perspective on the subject of elearning. We're going to include just about any use of computers, in all their many and various forms, to help people learn. We're happy to include, on the one hand, self-study lessons delivered on a PC, while also accommodating social learning conducted using mobile devices. We're as happy with online video as we are with the use of virtual classroom tools to deliver live group workshops. And while the primary focus of this book is on the use of elearning in the workplace, we understand that very similar applications can be found in schools, colleges and, indeed, the home.

Where does elearning come from?

The term elearning was first coined in October 1999, in a seminar run by a company called CBT Systems (now SkillSoft). At that time, it was quite an innovation to place the letter "e" in front of a verb to recognize the fact that here was an exciting new application of the Internet. Of course "e" actually stands for "electronic", which is a much more mundane and ambiguous term than, say, "online" or "digital", but electronic is what we have to work with.

In 1999, what CBT Systems was primarily referring to when it coined this new term was CBT (computer-based training) delivered not from a CD-ROM but over a network such as an organization's intranet or the global Internet. And CBT is what many people still consider to be what the term elearning really means. So what is CBT?

CBT is the delivery, by computer, of a self-paced lesson to an individual learner. Yes, just like so much elearning. The computer software takes the place of a teacher to carry out the task of instruction more efficiently (CBT is generally regarded as 50% faster than the equivalent classroom experience) and maybe more effectively (although this is much more difficult to prove).

So elearning is CBT delivered online. Well, it has many other forms as we shall see, but this application is worth sticking with for a moment, because it has a long history.

CBT originated in the mid-1970s, before we even had PCs. It was delivered using exotic and highly-expensive early mini-computers and workstations, and sometimes even on those green-screen terminals that connected you to a multi-million pound corporate mainframe. If you were to see one of those early CBT lessons, you would find the format surprisingly familiar. In fact, the self-study tutorial has remained fairly constant in shape and form over more than thirty years. It is ironic, perhaps, that many classroom instructors regard elearning as the new kid on the block, when in fact the careers of some of those working in elearning are longer than the complete lifetimes of the classroom trainers.

Some people think that modern elearning is much more interactive than it used to be "in the old days". Far from it. Interactivity with digital content uses a trivial amount of processing power and was well within the reach of the earliest computers. So, presumably early CBT was much less rich in terms of multimedia? Again, not so. True, early developers had to use all forms of complicated add-ons such as videodisc players and even computer-controllable VHS players to provide audio and video, but they did it just the same. In fact, the most popular term for what we now call elearning in the 1980s was "interactive video".

So elearning as a means for delivering self-paced lessons to individual learners is nothing new. In fact, many of the early CBT diehards can sometimes be every bit as resistant to change as their classroom counterparts. But elearning as of 2013 is a much richer medium than CBT and much more exciting. So what can you do with it now?

Why do so many people dislike elearning?

Actually, plenty of people like elearning a lot, but the problem is not really the medium, it is how it is used. If elearning is only used to deliver very dull, mandatory training then it is not surprising that many recipients of this training will be unhappy; this strategy would be unpopular however it was delivered.

Another potential problem is an over-reliance on self-study. This might be a highly flexible way to deliver a learning intervention, but it only really works in small doses – we are social animals and we like to engage with experts and with our peers. Luckily, elearning is not limited to self-study, as we demonstrate in this chapter.

What forms can elearning take?

Self-study lessons

For continuity, we should start this tour with the format that, as we've already discovered, was formerly known as CBT (actually it was known by many other three-letter acronyms and quite a few rude words as well, but let's not complicate things). CBT delivers a lesson to an individual learner at the learner's own pace. While this format is not new, it still has some important advantages:

- Learners like learning at their own pace, because this is generally less stressful. When you control the pace, you can take your time over the stuff you find difficult and zoom past anything that is old news to you or of little interest. You cannot do this in a classroom, even a virtual one. You're stuck with what all the other participants are getting.
- Learners like learning in small chunks and for good reason – you retain much more. One thing we have learned from cognitive neuroscience over the past ten years is just how easily learners can be overloaded. For the poor learner, many courses are like drinking from a fire hose. When you learn in small chunks, you can focus on a few key principles, reflect on these and hopefully put them into practice.
- Learners don't like to hang around waiting for the next scheduled course. With the instant access we have to information using tools such as Google, YouTube and Wikipedia, we've become accustomed to learning on-demand.

There are advantages for employers too:

- Large numbers of employees can be trained at the same time, which is particularly useful if you're rolling out a new system or policy.
- Assuming you have enough of an audience to justify the development cost, you will achieve massive economies of scale compared to instructor-led events.
- As we've already seen, self-study elearning is twice as fast as the classroom at achieving the same level of learning.

The intention of CBT was always that it would do as good a job as an instructor and in some respects this is true. It certainly delivers a more consistent product than an instructor and doesn't ever suffer from boredom, fatigue or hangovers. Well designed and it will be more clear, concise and rich in media. Where it scores less well is in the extent to which it can adapt to the needs of individual learners. Whether or not you believe in learning styles, we can safely say that all seven billion of us humans are different, and computers don't do as good a job as instructors at empathizing with our differences.

By and large, the discipline of artificial intelligence failed to deliver on its promise. Unfortunately, with its demise, we have seen little or no progress in the degree to which elearning materials are personalized around the unique characteristics of individual learners. We're still at the one size fits all stage.

Computers are capable of delivering highly adaptive, personalized learning, but in this respect we've hardly begun. It does not take rocket science to maintain a digital profile of each learner, in the same way a teacher does, and to use that information in simple ways: to point them to the material that is the most relevant, to suggest material that would remedy any problems they are encountering, to point the learner to next steps. Amazon does this, without an enormous amount of coding, so why not elearning developers?

Now there is a less complex option and that is simply to allow the learner the maximum amount of choice, to do whatever they want, however they want. And choice is a wonderful thing, but only to the extent that the learner has any idea of what it is that they don't know.

Simulations and virtual worlds

Some skills can only be practised in the real world and without a computer in sight. Other skills are much better rehearsed in the security of a virtual world, because that way there's no risk to reputation, bank balance, health and safety. Would you rather have the airline pilot who takes you on holiday practise on a simulator or in a real plane with passengers? The same goes for surgeons, lorry drivers, emergency workers, operators at nuclear power plants and those who work on oil rigs in the North Sea. They all perform tasks that entail high risks; it makes complete sense that they hone their skills and experience in the wide range of situations that could occur in the real world within the safety of one that is virtual.

Simulations allow people to learn from their mistakes without risk to life and limb and without embarrassment. They are at their most glamorous when they take place in highly-realistic 3D worlds, involving fast action and a hint of danger; but simulations can as easily be found on humble spreadsheets (for a financial simulation, say) or involve tasks no more dangerous than a sales interview. Simulations can be created with authoring tools but most commonly require a great deal of specialist expertise. Unless you are one of these specialists, your role is more likely to be in spotting the opportunity, defining the processes that the simulation needs to model, and helping to support implementation.

Another area of increasing potential is the use of multi-player virtual worlds, which allow participants to interact with each other online in a 3D environment. Technology like this has been used as an alternative to role-playing in a classroom, say to practise interpersonal situations in a retail store, or as a more practical and economic way of rehearsing how to deal with major incidents such as natural disasters, accidents and terrorist attacks. It may seem fanciful that your organization would ever make use of such technology, but remember that this is normal practice for players of online games.

Do I need to be technical to play a role in elearning?

Because elearning works with computers and networks there is a need for some people with specialist technical skills. However, most tasks in elearning require no more technical ability than you would expect from any office worker or competent home computer user. You don't have to be obsessed with technology but you do want to become its friend.

Virtual classrooms

To explain what a virtual classroom is we will have to introduce some words – "synchronous" and "asynchronous" – that you wouldn't normally use in polite company. We are not doing this for effect; it's just that these are the correct words for the job and are commonly used in elearning, so you may as well add them to your vocabulary.

Synchronous communication requires all participants to make themselves available at an agreed time. It's live and it's real-time. It can be contrasted with asynchronous communication, which frees up participants from the need to be available at the same time.

The principal synchronous elearning tool is web conferencing, which can be used to conduct live meetings, training sessions, briefings or presentations via the Internet. The extended functionality of web conferencing systems usually requires participants to download a special client application to their computers. This functionality includes online audio and video, application sharing, electronic whiteboards, shared media (such as PowerPoint presentations), text chat and polling. Most systems will also support voice communication using teleconferencing for those participants who don't have the hardware or the bandwidth to support online audio. Web conferencing systems include Cisco WebEx, Microsoft LiveMeeting, Saba Centra, Citrix GoToMeeting, Adobe Acrobat Connect and Blackboard Collaborate.

A "webinar" is an online seminar, lecture or presentation, delivered using web conferencing software. Webinars are good for sharing ideas and experiences, much like any typical session at a face-to-face conference. A live online learning event (or "virtual classroom" as it's often called) uses the same or similar software to facilitate learning. Of course you could also learn something from a webinar, but in the virtual classroom learning is the explicit purpose.

Learning together online is clearly more efficient than getting together face-to-face: it saves a large amount of money that would otherwise have been spent on travel and subsistence, not to mention all the wasted travelling time. Learning where you normally work is also more environmentally friendly, which has to be a good thing. It also encourages shorter sessions (how many workshops are padded out to last a full day?) and if some element of a session is not directly relevant to you, you can always do something else while you wait.

However, there are also circumstances in which you might get *more* effective results online than you could achieve face-to-face:

- Participants don't need to travel, which means you can arrange a session as soon as the need arises.
- You will find it easier to attract the participation of experts who are geographically distant from you. You may never get a specialist to travel across the world to contribute to your face-to-face event, but they will find it hard to object to making available an hour of their time online.
- Web conferencing allows a degree of anonymity, so introverts may find it easier to contribute than they would face-to-face.
- You can record sessions, so that those who miss a live event can catch up later.

As we've seen, communication can be synchronous or asynchronous, and when you design a learning intervention, you have the choice between the two. Given the advantages of being asynchronous – self-pacing, freedom over when you learn and for how long – there has to be a good reason for going synchronous. The following situations call out for a real-time response:

- When real-time interaction with experts is critical and participants must have questions answered before they can move on.
- When it is important for people to interact and share ideas concurrently.
- When the facilitator must be able to observe that participants have mastered a skill. By engaging in practical exercises in a live event, participants can demonstrate real-time skills and thinking.
- When a live event will help to ensure that a learning task is completed. Participants are more likely to carry out a self-paced task, such as reading or writing up an assignment, if they know a live event is coming up at which they will have to report on their progress. Nancy White describes how "synchronous events can provide a heartbeat for an on-going community, group or network. We put them on our agenda instead of saying 'I'll do that later' and they focus our attention."
- When conveying late-breaking and time-sensitive information.
- When there is a need to adjust the level or complexity of material in real-time based on the way participants are responding to the material.
- When questions and areas of difficulty cannot be easily predicted in advance.
- When there isn't the time or budget to develop asynchronous materials, such as self-paced elearning.
- When the presence of a trainer will contribute significantly to learning. As Jonathan Finkelstein reports: "People need not be present concurrently with an

instructor to simply have information passed on to them, yet the active construction of knowledge by learners through a process of real-time give and take is well served in a live online setting."

- When a guest expert is available for a limited time only and couldn't respond to questions in a forum over a longer period.

While virtual classrooms are a mainstay in many multinational and geographically-dispersed organizations, they are still a complete mystery to others. We can expect to see a major pick-up in the use of web conferencing for learning as time, budgetary and environmental pressures make live, face-to-face communication a luxury for special events only.

Online resources

Interactivity can contribute a great deal to learning:

- It helps to focus the learner's attention (important when you consider the millions of sensory stimuli to which the brain is exposed every day).
- By working with new ideas and information, it encourages the formation of new connections in long-term memory (which is necessary if a learner is going to retain anything that they learn).
- Through reinforcement, rehearsal and practice, it makes it easier for the learner to recall what they have learned when they need it.

So interaction is absolutely vital then. But this interactivity can be achieved in a number of different ways:

- By working with instructors, experts, coaches and peers – asking and answering questions, providing each other with feedback, practising together, discussing different perspectives, and so on.
- By interacting with the learning content itself, as you would with the self-study materials and simulations that we discussed above.
- By the efforts of the learner alone, reflecting, making notes and trying things out. Yes, we can learn without third-party intervention, as anyone who's ever benefited from reading a book, listening to a radio programme or watching a film or TV documentary can attest. And that's all of us, right?

If we doubt whether online learning materials can be effective without being interactive, then we don't have far to look for evidence. Can we honestly say that huge
learning gains are not being made from resources such as YouTube or Wikipedia?
Clearly what are essentially passive resources can stimulate a great deal of learning,
sometimes within a formal context, such as a course, but also quite incidentally as
part of our everyday lives.

Online learning resources can take many forms:

- Web articles
- Videos
- Podcasts
- PDF files (useful when a document needs to be printed)
- Slide shows, perhaps with narration so they can stand alone without a presenter
- Screencasts (simple software demos).

And the great thing about content like this is that you don't necessarily have to be an
expert to put it together. While not everybody fancies themselves as a writer, artist
or director, plenty of people can do a good enough job when it comes to sharing
their experiences and ideas. We've already mentioned Wikipedia and YouTube, and
both of these depend on content being contributed from the bottom up, by users
and enthusiasts. You'll never be able to meet every learning need by publishing formal content on a top-down basis, so don't think of this as competition, just making
sure the job gets done.

Online collaboration

We may have started this guided tour with the more familiar forms of elearning but
we're going to finish with what could turn out to be the most significant of all. We
only have to look at the World Wide Web to see how it has developed in the twenty
years since Sir Tim Berners-Lee introduced it to the world, when he worked at the
European Centre for Nuclear Research in Geneva.

Although there were exceptions, the majority of early web sites were essentially col-
lections of published documents – useful true, but the user was primarily a con-
sumer, as they were when they read the newspaper or watched TV. Web 2.0 – the
read-write Web – changed all that. Our experience of the Web now is primarily

interactive. Whether it's on eBay, Facebook or an online dating site, the Web brings people together as much as it helps people to find content.

Although our interactive online experiences have brought major changes in our lives outside work, it would be fair to say that we have yet to see significant evidence of a similar phenomenon in our 9 to 5 existence. The tools we use to interact with our friends – social networks, blogs, Twitter and so on – are often denied us at work, when we could similarly benefit from interacting with our colleagues.

This is changing, albeit slowly, but the increased expectations of a generation weaned on a diet of constant peer interaction will certainly have its effect in time, and more and more managers who were brought up to expect rigid hierarchical communication will themselves get the message through their own forays into social media and, vicariously, through those of their children. Learning professionals themselves have to contemplate change, as their role as primary information provider is clearly no longer sustainable. The trainer of the future won't be doing so much training; they're as likely to be a coach, a content creator and a curator. We will almost certainly look back in 10–15 years to see this period as a crossroads, as we experience the first real revolution in workplace learning.

In the meantime, there are plenty of organizations, which are making use of social learning within the more formal context of blended learning courses, using forums for group discussions, blogs as a means for reflective learning and wikis for group tasks. It's a step in the right direction.

Does elearning work?

Of course it all depends on what form of elearning you are talking about – self-study lessons, virtual classrooms, online resources, simulations, online collaboration. Each has its own particular strengths and weaknesses.

What use is elearning?

We've looked so far at the forms that elearning can take, but what really matters is what you can achieve with all these options. One way to achieve this is by looking at the most common educational and training strategies and seeing, in each case, how learning technologies could help:

Exposition

Exposition is the delivery of information from teacher or subject expert to learner. It's as simple as that. Exposition is essentially a one-way process, although it may include some modest Q&A or discussion. The strategy is top-down and teacher-centred because it is the person designing and/or delivering who determines what information is to be delivered and how (and sometimes also where and when).

Exposition can take place in the context of an *event*, such as a lecture, a seminar or a presentation. Historically most learning events have been delivered face-to-face, but there are powerful arguments for using web conferencing to allow more people to participate at less cost and without concern for geographical location.

Exposition can also take the form of *content*. The classic medium for expositional content is, of course, the printed book, although various other forms of "offline media", including tapes, CDs and DVDs, have extended the possibilities to include audio and video. Now most content is consumed online or downloaded for delivery on portable platforms such as iPods, tablets and e-book readers.

Instruction

Instruction, the second strategy, is still a teacher/trainer-centred approach, but is much more carefully crafted to ensure that the learning outcomes are actually achieved, regardless of the learner's ability. In this sense it is process rather than subject-matter driven. This process depends on the explicit and up-front definition of learning objectives and then the careful selection of appropriate activities and resources that will enable those objectives to be achieved.

The process of 'instructional design' is teacher/trainer-centred because it focuses on learning objectives rather than learner goals; on the other hand, the fact that instruction is typically an interactive rather than a passive learner experience, means that the process can be adaptive to some degree to the individual differences of particular learners.

Like exposition, instruction can take the form of a live event or of content. Instructional events can take place in the workplace – what we normally call 'on-job training' – or in a classroom. These experiences can be successfully replicated online in a virtual classroom.

Instruction can also take the form of self-study lessons. While these may have been delivered historically in a rather limited form through workbooks, much more effective results can be achieved with self-paced elearning.

Guided discovery

The third strategy, guided discovery, has many similarities with instruction in that it is very much a structured and facilitated process, but it follows a very different sequence of events.

While instruction moves from theory to practice, from the general to the specific, guided discovery starts with the specific and moves to the general. It is an *inductive* process – it leads the learner towards insights and generalizations, rather than providing these on a plate. Because this process is much less certain and predictable, guided discovery rarely has specific learning objectives – every learner will take out of the process something unique and personal. What they take out will depend not only on the insights they gain from the particular learning experience, but also to a great deal on their prior knowledge and previous life experience.

Guided discovery can take many forms – experiments in a laboratory, simulations, scenarios, case studies or team-building activities. In each of these cases, the learner is presented, alone or in a group, with a task to accomplish. Having undertaken that task, the learner is then encouraged to reflect on the experience – what went well, what less well? How could the successes be repeated and the failures avoided? The conclusions can be taken forward to further exercises and then hopefully applied to real-world tasks.

As we have seen, elearning can play a key role in guided discovery, through the use of simulations and scenarios, providing opportunities that could be difficult or even impossible to replicate in a classroom.

Guided discovery can also take place in a more informal, on-job setting, a good example of which is coaching. The role of the coach is to help the learner to reflect on their real-world experiences, gain insights and make new generalizations that can be tested out on future tasks. While most coaching is conducted face-to-face, there are plenty of possibilities for online coaching using tools such as Skype, web conferencing or even email.

Exploration

Exploration is by far the most learner-centred of the four strategies and the only one that relies on the learner to make all the choices. It also represents the closing of the circle, because as with exposition, the first strategy we looked at, the learning design is both simple and relatively unstructured, in stark contrast to instruction and guided discovery.

With the exploration strategy, each learner determines their own learning process, taking advantage of resources provided not only by teachers and trainers but also by peers. What they take out of this process is entirely individual and largely unpredictable. As such, exploration may seem a relatively informal strategy, but no less useful for that. In fact it's probably the way that a great deal of learning takes place.

Exploration may play a small part in a formal course, perhaps a handout, a job aid or a list of books or links, which learners can dip into if they wish. On the other hand, it could just as easily form the basis for a complete just-in-time performance support system in the workplace.

Online materials already provide hundreds of millions of people with the resources they need to learn – or at the very least to acquire information – as and when they wish. Almost anyone who is computer-literate now turns to Google, YouTube or Wikipedia to answer a question or follow up an interest.

The exploration strategy is further enhanced by collaboration with experts and other learners, through forums, wikis, blogs, Twitter and social networks. With billions of people connected to the Internet, someone who shares your interests or can answer your question will never be far away.

Table 1.1 *Elearning across four educational and training strategies*

	Exposition	Instruction	Guided discovery	Exploration
Online events	Webinars/ webcasts	Virtual class- room sessions	E-coaching	
Online content	Podcasts/e- books/videos/ web articles/ PDFs	Self-paced elearning	Simulations/ scenarios	Performance support materials/videos/ screencasts/web articles/PDFs
Online collaboration				Forums/blogs/wikis/ social networks

Does elearning spell the end for the classroom trainer?

Elearning is disruptive to the status quo, as you would expect with such a major new approach, and it is completely realistic to expect there to be less delivery in the classroom – in fact this has already happened. However, the skills of the trainer will still be needed in the virtual classroom, in moderating collaborative learning experiences and in the creation of learning resources. The role will change, certainly, but it will always be needed.

Moving on

On the one hand, elearning can be seen as not such a big deal: just another medium for the delivery of learning content and just another channel through which teachers and learners can interact. But, as we have seen, this is a particularly versatile medium, capable of delivering a high quality and highly-adaptive multimedia experience on a wide range of devices and with unprecedented scalability.

It is true that there are circumstances in which elearning cannot adequately replace the face-to-face learning experience, but this is not a major concern. Elearning is not the answer to every problem but it is the answer to many. It can be happily blended with more traditional approaches, so we achieve the best of both worlds. All that is needed is an open mind and an active imagination.

Laura Overton is the Managing Director of Towards Maturity – a not-for-profit benchmark practice that provides independent research to help business deliver improved performance through learning innovation.

Laura established the Towards Maturity Benchmark to help organizations learn from each other's successes. Over the last 10 years, 2,500 organizations have used the benchmark to help them establish an effective e-enabled learning culture.

Laura was the author of "Linking Learning To Business" – one of the first industry benchmark studies with both organizations and learners investigating good practices (January 2004). Since then she has authored over 20 independent reports sharing benchmarks and effective practices to drive performance which are referenced around the globe.

With over two decades of experience of implementing learning technologies in the workplace, she has worked with government policy makers representing employer interests and sits on the steering committee of a number of industry boards. Her work has been recognized through a number of special achievement awards.

LinkedIn: lauraoverton
Twitter: @lauraoverton
Website: www.towardsmaturity.org/benchmarking
   www.towardsmaturity.org/learner

One of the biggest challenges is making the case for elearning and blended learning to senior managers. They may be attracted by the cost savings but if they go for the cheapest option, will it be effective (more for less)? The purpose of this chapter is to arm you with the research, arguments and case studies that make the case for the *right* sort of elearning. It will also share practical tips for demonstrating the value of elearning and the effect it can have on an organization's bottom line.

What's the big idea?

The change in culture and engaging with staff is a far bigger issue than the technology. If you get that right you've cracked it!

We've got a big agenda for learning technologies in the workplace! On average 20% of a dwindling L&D budget is being invested in learning technology with increasingly high expectations of return. Over 9 out of 10 organizations from across the private, public and not-for-profit sectors around the globe are looking to deliver value, harness talent and know-how, and improve business agility without compromising the quality of the learning experience.[1]

There is an increasing thirst for change in the way we deliver learning and support performance in the workplace. But if we are to be champions for change, we need to take a step back from a world of technologies and pedagogies that excite us and step into the world of business and performance that excites our most influential stakeholders.

If we want senior managers to engage with change and release finance to support new ways of learning, we need to give them motive.

If we want to deliver value, we need to understand what value looks like for our organizations.

If we want to fully engage busy staff members we need to find new ways of supporting them in their day-to-day challenges.

In short if we want to get the business on board with new ways of learning, we have to first get on board with the ways of business!

This chapter is all about setting realistic expectations and bringing our organizations with us as we go. If we want to see sustainable change in the way that learning is delivered, we have to win the hearts and minds of the people that matter.

If we can do this, we will create a firm foundation for lasting elearning effectiveness in our organizations that is not reliant on the latest technology fad or whim.

This chapter outlines how you can connect with the people that matter and establish those foundations for future success.

Give me the details

Ensure that you have a clear understanding of who your stake-holders are and what their interest is in the project, miss someone and it can be very costly later on.

We all have the desire to get our business on board with learning for their good as well as ours. We need senior execs to back our programmes, line managers to release and support individuals and for the individuals themselves to commit to changing their behaviour as a result of our interventions. Life would be so much easier if they just "got it"!

The trouble is, we are hampered by history. Businesses' traditional view of learning and development is that it is a function that reacts to demand "I have a problem, I must need a course". So L&D provides events and elearning programmes in a response to that demand, but ultimately the business perceives L&D as being a non-essential cost centre with a focus on courses rather than a partner with a shared focus on the performance of the business. And this makes it tricky for us to harness elearning in new ways and to exploit its full potential to encourage sharing, support performance and deliver faster, smarter learning opportunities.

But times are changing. 9 out of 10 L&D professionals in our 2012-13 benchmark recognize the importance of integrating learning into the workflow – it's no longer just

Top 10 drivers for investing in learning technologies in 2013:

1. Increase learning access and flexibility 98%
2. Increase the ongoing sharing of good practice 95%
3. Improve the quality of learning delivered 94%
4. Speed up and improve the application of learning back in workplace 94%
5. Increase consistency of learning experience 93%
6. Deliver greater value for money 93%
7. Improve management and administration of learning at work 93%
8. Reduce time to competence 92%
9. Provide a faster response to changing business conditions 92%
10. Improve talent/performance management 91%

Data from 500 respondents in the 2012-13 Towards Maturity Benchmark Study.

Figure 2.1   *Top 10 drivers for investing in elearning*

about creating great courses but getting up close and personal. And, as you can see from Figure 2.1, we have high expectations of learning technology to help us in this journey. But we need more than just technology – to do this effectively we need to win the hearts and minds of the business stakeholders in the organizations that we support.

Over 2,500 organizations have participated in the Towards Maturity Benchmark Study since 2003 from across private, public and not-for-profit sectors. We've found that success is driven by innovative thinking and business partnerships, not learning technology. Those that are more mature in their approach to implementation are three to four times more likely to report improved productivity, customer satisfaction and ability to respond faster to business change as a result of their learning approaches.

So what are the mature users doing differently? The Benchmark has isolated a number of organizational behaviours and processes consistently shown in top performing organizations. These are tracked and measured using the Towards Maturity Index, a unique indicator that measures the level of effective practices in an organization. The index allows us to isolate the top 25% of the participants in order to identify what separates out the top performers from the rest.

We've found that maturity does not necessarily relate to organization size or to the length of time that they have been using learning technologies. However, we find

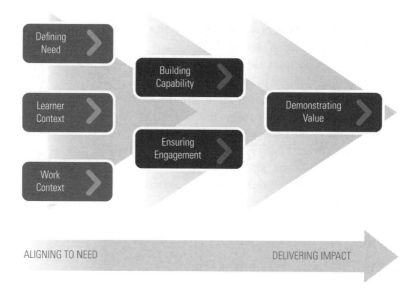

Figure 2.2   *The towards maturity model*

that those that are more mature consistently engage in six workstreams of good practice (see Figure 2.2) which are at the heart of the Towards Maturity Index.

What sets the top performers apart is their focus on alignment to need and delivering value back to the organization. They achieve this through proactive stakeholder engagement, not through technology platforms and tools

Who are our influential stakeholders?

Top learning companies have identified a number of different stakeholders who influence success:

Learners: In Learning and Development, we support a varied audience but in the main they are nurses, care workers, financial advisors, new marketing people, IT professionals, secretaries – they are not students or course participants and it's important to remember their day job when we seek to engage them.

Senior business leaders: Our stakeholders also include our learners' bosses, project managers and those responsible for rolling out new systems and processes. Our learning solutions need to solve their problems if we are to add value.

Line managers: In the original Towards Maturity Learning Landscape study we found that 55% of 3,000 learners said that the person most likely to influence them to learn online would be their line managers (less than 1 in 10 said anyone linked to HR and training!). They are often forgotten, but it's important that we work out how to help line managers support their staff better.

Project leaders and functional heads: These guys are responsible for implementing new initiatives, new processes or systems, new IT systems or product lines for the organization. They set the priority for timing and resourcing and yet often forget to engage with learning until the last minute.

The IT department: If you want your technology-enabled solutions to take off it's always a good idea to be best friends with the IT department. Find out what your IT infrastructure is capable of – there may be technology platforms in place that can be leveraged for learning and performance support but you won't know if you don't ask!

Trainers: Top learning companies don't underestimate the role of the traditional trainer in influencing change. The classroom can be a great place to introduce new ways of learning!

Local Learning Champions: Local enthusiasts and power users, who understand the issues and politics on the ground, can be incredible assets to a successful roll-out of new learning approaches.

HR and Organizational Development colleagues: It is worthwhile considering how learning can be integrated into existing talent management and organizational development policies. Too often HR functions work in isolation but top learning companies are working at bringing down the internal silos to create a seamless journey for the staff members to progress their skills and their career.

Take time out to create a stakeholder map by asking the questions:

- Who is most likely to influence the success of my elearning project?
- Who is most interested in the success of my elearning project?

Use this map to identify and then connect with those with the most influence and the most interest!

So how do I do it?

Building the business case

It's worth trying to convince yourself about the benefits.

Doing your research

What is keeping your stakeholders awake at night?

This is one of the most critical questions we can ask at the beginning of our elearning journey if we want to engage the most influential people in our business. When you seriously consider this question, you can bet that it won't be anything to do with learning, training or learning technologies!

Only 50% of us analyse the business need before recommending a learning solution. Yet those organizations who do and also involve business leaders in setting the priorities for learning at the start, get better buy-in and take-up of their learning initiative than those who don't. Understanding how learning contributes to the business's objectives can help you make a strong case and win hearts and minds before you even begin.

It is worth doing your research internally to help you find your answers. Your annual report or results of your latest employee or customer study all provide excellent insights into the concerns of senior managers. And it is not just about the bottom line, research from the ASTD and IBM in 2006 highlighted that senior executives' perception of value is really important. With executives' desire to have engaged employees in the workplace, they are just as interested in the intangible evidence, for example, that confidence has increased.

They are more likely to be concerned with questions like:

- How can I increase customer loyalty?
- How can I ensure that our organization is first to market?
- How do we improve both service and efficiency?
- How can we ensure we have the right talent in place to take this organization forward?
- How do I ensure our organization is compliant?

Than questions like:

- How much money will I save?
- How can I increase course completions?

Don't take my word for it, Richard Beaven, the Customer Services Director, General Insurance at Lloyds Bank comments in the foreword of our 2012-13 report:

> "We can't afford to obsess about the latest learning technology delivery vehicles. Successful organizations are using technology to apply innovative learning solutions to important business problems . . . The best outcomes for learning will be delivered by a learning team who deeply understand business strategy and the required business outcomes."

The issues keeping both line managers and their staff awake at night may be different. It is worth asking one additional question to find out how we can best support them:

- How can I help you to do your job better?

I encourage you to mine the great resources available to help you uncover the needs in your business but once you have understood them, it's also important to identify if elearning actually help you to address them.

Can elearning help?

If you are new to elearning, it's difficult to make the business case for doing things differently without some strong evidence to show that your new approach will have an effect.

That's when it is worth doing your research outside of the company. For the last three years Towards Maturity have been independently gathering evidence to help you build your business case. Over a period of 30 months, 700 organizations volunteered evidence of the impact that learning technologies are having on the bottom line of their business and on learning efficiency. Figure 2.3 outlines the evidence we've gathered. Not everyone is looking for the same results but a considerable number of organizations have now conservatively quantified the benefits so that you can build a better business case.

Evidence of success
Study time reduced by 29%
Delivery time reduced by 25%
Increase in programme reach by 25%
Cost reduced by 22%
Time to competency reduced by 22%
Customer satisfaction improved by 16%
Ability to change procedures or products improved by 22%
Efficiency in demonstrating compliance is improved by 33%
Ability to speed up the rollout of new IT applications improved by 24%
Qualifications increased by 17%
Staff satisfaction/engagement has improved by 16%
Staff attrition rates reduced by 9%

Figure 2.3   *Bottom-line benefits of learning technologies*

How can you use these figures?

Consider answering the following questions for your organization:

- If I can reduce delivery time by 25% what would that mean for the outputs of our training staff?
- What will it mean to my hospital ward, my sales team or my volunteers if I can get a new member of staff up to speed a fifth quicker than before?
- What competitive advantage will we have if we can release a new product or process 22% quicker?
- What will be the impact on recruitment costs if we reduce staff attrition by 9%?
- What if we can do this and reduce training costs by 22%?

Would your business leaders be interested in these arguments? We think so!

In fact top learning companies in the Towards Maturity Benchmark are doing their research before designing their solutions. They are:

- 50% more likely than average to analyse the business need before recommending a solution.

- Twice as likely to identify specific business metrics that they want to improve through learning in partnership with senior management.
- Nearly three times as likely to involve learners, line managers and even trainers in the design phase of creating the solution itself.

Getting your message out

Advertise, advertise, advertise the advantages to all.

The steps involved in winning over senior leaders are critical to secure budget and resources, and to make sure that the projects you are involved in actually meet the needs of those we want to engage with. But once we've developed our programmes, we need to let people know what is available and continually encourage them to come back for more. We are in danger of creating great programmes but then not telling people about them.

Only 2 out of 5 organizations are confident that their staff can access clear information on the learning available to them.

If we want our staff and their managers to engage with elearning, they have to know what is available to them and what the benefits will be. It sounds obvious doesn't it but in reality only 40% of organizations are proactive in putting a communications plan in place for all their key stakeholders. Top performers on the other hand are not as shy. They are almost twice as likely to be focusing on the critical task of continually raising awareness.

Putting a communications plan in place doesn't have to be a tough task. Here are some practical steps to help you get started:

Know your audience (it's worth repeating this one!)

Map out the most influential stakeholders for your project and what is keeping them awake at night so that you can adapt your communication message for each one, for example:

- Managers might be interested in their staff having less time out of business.
- Function heads want to see improved business efficiency.

- Learners want to know what's in it for them – job development, career enhancement, self-enrichment?
- Executives need feedback on the bottom-line results.

Be clear about what you want to achieve

Think about the communication message for each audience:

- Have a clear objective about what you want to achieve with your communication. Do you want recipients to increase their awareness, to get information, to be motivated to act?
- Keep the message relevant (to their needs not yours) and simple.
- If you want your communications to stick, don't be afraid to repeat yourself through different media but be consistent in your message (for example look-and-feel and vocabulary).
- Don't try to make too many points – you'll only dilute your core messages.
- Be clear about the next steps that you want them to take and how to take them.

Mix media for maximum effect

When life and work are so busy, it is rare that you will reach everyone with just one communication. It is critical to repeat your message from different angles. There are a number of routes to bring your communication message to your audience. Marketers will think of these in terms of advertising, sales promotions, public relations, using a direct sale force and direct marketing. Table 2.1 highlights how L&D departments can use some of these tools in the promotion of learning:

Use a combination of these tools to communicate frequently with staff. Once you start to see results, share them widely to stimulate more interest. For example you could consider how to share peer testimonies through video, interviews, or even a poster campaign. It's not just your learners who like to hear from each other's experience, managers want to know what other managers are doing. Senior execs will often act on the recommendation of other senior leaders. League tables are also very powerful in capturing the attention of competitive managers who don't want to be left behind!

Leverage resources and expertise around you

Marketing might not be your field of expertise but there are plenty of people around you that could help:

Table 2.1 *Example promotional tools for trainers*

Advertising	Sales Promotions	Public Relations	Sales Force	Direct Marketing
Packaging and logos for example for induction	Competitions	In-house magazines	Elearning champions	Email with direct links
	Giveaways	External press coverage	Managers	SMS
Posters	Road shows		Toolkits for champions and managers	Flyers in pay slips
Literature, flyers and leaflets	Demonstrations	Awards		Banners on the intranet
Rolling PowerPoint presentations	League tables	Peer-to-peer sharing of success stories		Internal YouTube or social media sites
	Team briefings			
	Teaser campaigns			

- Internal marketing and communications departments can provide advice, design expertise and resources.
- Vendors can sometimes share best practice, help you offer giveaways (for example, they might provide you with gifts such as pens to pass on to your learners). They can also help you to quantify learning results.

Timing is everything

- Don't communicate until you know the technology works!
- Consider if there are other initiatives about to be launched that will either enhance or hinder your communications.
- Don't stop communicating – there will always be someone who missed it the first time around.

Think wider than your own organization

External recognition is a powerful internal motivator. Top performers are twice as likely to be entering external awards and then using their successes to further promote internally. Why not consider a bit of external PR to help you with your communication strategies:

- Internal newsletters and external industry journals and newsletters are often looking for interesting new stories (but don't forget to check with your PR department first!).

- Communicate internally any external recognition of best practice, for example award wins and published case studies, as this helps to build internal credibility.

Equip your local champions with the tools they need

You can't be everywhere at once – particularly in large global companies it is important to identify local champions to help you communicate locally. But it is important to support them properly:

- Create centralized resources that others can use and tailor, offer implementation guidelines to help save them time.
- Encourage local champions to share their own resources and success stories to inspire others around the organization.

Demonstrating value

> Don't give up. Always be ready to offer that technology solution – the need will likely come out of nowhere and you've got to be ready to seize your chance to demonstrate your solution's value.

Thanks to the input from the key stakeholders you've designed a relevant project and, as a result of your communication strategy, there has been lots of engagement – we are off to a great start. But how successful have we been?

The one area where organizations are likely to fall down is demonstrating value back to the original stakeholders. Top learning companies understand that success breeds success and are more likely to be gathering feedback, measuring impact AND communicating successes back to those that matter.

There are some great evaluation models available now to help us understand the value that we are adding back to the business. Most are familiar with the four levels of learning evaluation proposed by Kirkpatrick (and extended to a fifth return on investment (ROI) level by Jack Phillips) – see Table 2.2. In times of economic uncertainty when organizations have to account more carefully for their budget and are looking for demonstrable value for money, it is surprising that so few of us

Table 2.2 *How are we evaluating our learning?*

Evaluation levels	What we found:
Level 1 – Reaction Did they Like it?	Most of us love the happy sheet! In fact 76% of organizations are using online surveys and questionnaires to help understand learner reaction.
Level 2 – Evidence of Learning Did they Learn it?	Only 25% routinely collect information on the extent to which learning points have been understood.
Level 3 – Behaviour or Skills Transfer Did they Use it back on the job?	Only 35% routinely collect information from learners on the extent to which the learning points have been applied at work.
Level 4 – Business Impact or Results Did it have an Impact on targeted outcomes?	Only 17% measure specific business metrics when evaluating the impact of learning technologies.
Level 5 – ROI Results Did it achieve measurable monetary Return on Investment?	Only 18% calculate Return on Investment for their learning programmes.

are actually measuring impact of our programmes beyond the basic "happy sheet" (level 1 evaluation of 'do you like it?').

The top performers are twice as likely to engage in levels 2–5 of these evaluation activities.

Many organizations base their assessment of benefits on anecdote, estimate and perception, all of which are helpful. We've found that those who dig deeper in calculating monetary returns actually report more benefits than the average. Those who evaluate their technology-enabled learning programmes with a full return on investment process benefit from more cost reduction, more productivity increases and speedier change programmes than those who are reporting benefits based on hearsay or best guesses (see Figure 2.4).

We may be doing ourselves a disservice in not measuring our impact more fully, so how can we get smarter in getting closer to the bottom line? When time is of the essence, how do we focus on what is important?

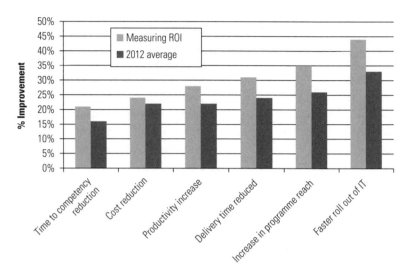

Figure 2.4 *How measuring return on investment increases improvement*

Begin with the results in mind

We've already discussed the importance of working in partnership with your stake-holders and agreeing up front with them what success looks like for your online learning solution (and don't be fobbed off with "I just want you to develop me a course"!) This is the most important part of the process as you now have a sense of:

- What **tangible** benefits you are looking for, for example a measurable improvement in quality (accidents reduced, tasks completed) or a reduction in costs or time (call resolution time decreased, or projects delivered faster) or even agreeing improvement in outputs (faster installation of a piece of kit or more sales).
- What **intangible** benefits you are looking for, for example in a change of work habits (such as absenteeism, communication), new skills, more staff development opportunities, new ideas generated or improved confidence.

Work with your stakeholder partners to place a monetary value on any tangible bene-fits uncovered. For example if your stakeholders are in agreement that you've been able to shave off two weeks from a learning programme, ask them to help you quantify how much those two weeks were worth to them in, for example, improved sales or reducing the cost of covering that person with a temp. If attrition has dropped by 3%, ask them to help you understand the implications on the recruitment bill for the organization.

Monitor and review against agreed outcomes

Over 90% of us are using online surveys and questionnaires in our elearning and with some slight adaptions we can make them more useful. Don't forget to use focus groups as well to keep in touch with how you are doing. In both, you need to balance the questions that you are asking:

- Ask more questions that uncover value – for example "How do you intend to apply this course?", "How much more confident do you feel as a result?" Or three months later, "How much time do you think you have saved as a result of . . .?"
- Ask fewer questions about ease of use – these might be useful questions to you to help you tweak the programme but they do not help you demonstrate the value you are adding to the business.

Don't forget to think about cost savings

One area that learning technologies have traditionally contributed to is cost savings and efficiency, although it is critical to remember that we should always balance efficiency savings with results. That said, only one in four organizations actually know the opportunity costs of their various learning approaches. This is a simple measure that is within our control:

- How much is our learning technology solution costing us?
- How much would this cost us in the classroom?

It is important to fully consider the cost of learning technologies to avoid hyping-up the numbers – for example include staff costs such as development time, administration time, and don't forget ongoing maintenance fees and support costs.

Communicate successes

Regularly feed your results back to those that matter – the findings from your evaluation process should be fed back into your overall communication strategy.

Hints and tips

We've covered a number of practical suggestions to help you build the business case and maintain engagement. Each year we also ask our benchmark participants about the practical hints and tips that they would like to pass on to their colleagues.

Their comments provide a perspective on how they have made their case for elearning. Here are just a few of their hints and tips gathered in the last two years:

Engage before executing:
- "Agree measures of success first with your stakeholders before adopting or designing any training, whether it be online or face-to-face."
- "Include the business [in] the design, be bold with your ideas, get buy-in from your audience by having ambassadors/advocates to help spread the word."
- "Buy-in from the top is essential. Start small and have measured results of how the new technologies can and have helped. Understand the company strategy and what the key areas of focus are. [Align] the introduction of the new technologies to these."

Connect with the people that matter:
- "Get more staff in the front line to make suggestions for improvements rather than the top down approach. Happier staff, saving time and money contribute to a healthier organization all round."
- "Don't over plan things and make sure you test ideas out with the people who'll use it, rather than just with people who you know will support you."
- "We continue to concentrate our efforts with stakeholders who have the appetite to work with us in a certain area. This is particularly so with social media and mobile learning, where we find that a lack of understanding hinders progress, but where we've made great strides with those who already 'get it'."

Walking a mile in their shoes:
- "Learning technologies are interesting for L&D. When this is not the main focus of the business, do not expect management to share the same enthusiasm."
- "Find out exactly what your Executives want from learning technologies as this will be different from Managers and employees."

Adding real business value:
- "Key one for me is to understand exactly what skills, experience and knowledge are crucial for our success. It's easy to get distracted from this and focus energy and funds on creating something sophisticated when a pragmatic, elegant solution is all that's needed."
- "Just because you are excited about learning technology doesn't mean everyone else will be. It has to add value to every individual that connects with it otherwise it will die."

Don't forget the IT department:
- "Treat IT as your partners, not the enemy. Ask if certain tech can be used and what alternatives may be more appropriate."
- "It's much easier to get the IT function's attention when something is not working if business leaders are using the tools for themselves!"

Getting started:
- "Be patient and kind with those showing resistance to new ways of learning. They will become your biggest and best advocates."
- "Don't go for big bang roll-outs of online learning. Keep it modest, simple and relevant to the business."
- "When we first launched el we decided not to go for a 'big bang' approach. We almost introduced elearning by stealth. As el became more and more accepted we have done a lot more to promote it. This has served us really well and there is no doubt that el is now a part of our L&D culture. The downside of this approach is that staff have not always been aware of what is available to them. With hindsight we would have adopted a more robust approach to communications."

Communicate Communicate Communicate:
- "You can never do too much promotion, senior managers need to buy into it, line managers must be committed to allow staff the time to complete."

When all else fails:
- "Take the initiative – ask forgiveness rather than permission!"

The usual suspects

Far too many workplace learning technology projects fail, far too frequently. Everyone has an unofficial war story of "where it all went wrong" but very few are willing to talk about it. A couple of years ago we detoured from looking at the behaviours of the successful and turned our attention to what we could learn from failed projects instead. We identified 33 reasons why elearning projects fail and 18 out of the 33 were linked to poor stakeholder engagement (the others were linked to poor implementation skills – something that this book will go on to address!)

Here are some specific danger zones to avoid when it comes to winning hearts and minds:

Mind your language

The language with all clients should be about their business and not about your learning technology.

When you are working on your communications plan, watch your language! Talk about what is important to your business and your learners not the latest features of your online learning!

Mandated training does not equal take-up

Simply mandating the completion of a learning stream within a given timescale can, and does, alienate learners to the detriment of future programmes.

Just because a course is mandated doesn't mean that people will do it! We've found that less than two thirds of targeted audiences complete compulsory training allocated to them – this varies from sector to sector but even in the Finance sector where it is business critical to meet the needs of the regulatory bodies, we only see four out of five individuals completing their compulsory industry learning. It is as critical, some would say more critical, to invest in designing engaging and attractive compliance content and to market and communicate its availability.

The dangers of labelling learners

Nearly two thirds of our benchmark participants do not believe that their staff have the necessary skills to manage their own learning and half state that user reluctance is still a barrier. But how much do we really know about our learners? I hear lots of comments about "our managers are technophobic" or "our young people might be willing to share information with each other but our older staff members won't". The trouble is that most of us base our views on anecdotal reactions to our current learning offerings mixed in with external information about learning styles or generational differences. Our evidence from our own Learning Landscape study with a number of organizations suggests that this is not the case. For example, it's not just the younger generations who are keen on sharing what they know, we've found that four out of five staff members (of all ages) say they would be willing to use technology to share information with colleagues if they had the opportunity. It makes life easier to label our staff and put them into convenient boxes, but everyone is different. There is a real danger that we base our decisions on what we think our learners want rather than actually checking out what they will find useful.

Overstating the benefits

It is very easy to be swayed by compelling arguments about efficiency, and it is very easy to create fantastic Return on Investment calculations that show cost benefits compared to the classroom, particularly when volumes of staff are involved. Too often I have seen organizations show that they have placed thousands of students through an elearning programme that would have cost millions if it had been completed face-to-face. This type of efficiency demonstration is just not credible – for several reasons:

- No organization would have spent millions on that programme in the first place so the comparison is not valid.
- Without proof of additional value add from the elearning experience, any experienced executive could (and should) ask – wouldn't it have been cheaper just to do nothing?

It is better to focus on credible figures and comparisons like the ones considered earlier in this chapter, better still to work with the executives themselves to articulate the value you are adding to the organization through your efficient approaches.

Focus on outputs not inputs!

Learning management systems are great for creating evidence. They can provide statistics of training hours, cost per access, resource allocation and course completions but are these evidence of improved business performance? These are all training input measures rather than output measures. They may be compelling statistics for training and development professionals but are of little interest to business stakeholders who are more likely to be interested in competition, costs, customer service and quality than courses, completions and hours spent learning.

It's a wrap

When embarking on your elearning journey (or kick starting it again once you have stalled), remember to engage before executing!

Your success will come when your programmes are used, your communities are supporting staff at their point of need, ideas are being shared and new skills are being applied. Technology provides so many opportunities to accelerate these results but the people will drive your success (or otherwise), not the technology.

We'd like to leave the last word to one of our Benchmark participants:

> *Engage with your customer; communicate effectively; deliver quality and champion the business benefits.*

Note

1. Towards Maturity has been independently researching effective elearning implementation practices since 2003. Unless stated otherwise, specific figures quoted will all be from the 2012–13 Towards Maturity Benchmark Study. All hints and tips and quotes are from the top learning companies who took part in the study. The full report can be downloaded at www.towardsmaturity.org/2012benchmark.

3. Build In-House, Buy Off-the-Shelf or Outsource?

· Jane Bozarth ·

DIY

COURSE

articulate

Dr **Jane Bozarth** is an internationally known trainer, instructional designer, author and speaker. Currently serving as eLearning Coordinator for the state of North Carolina, USA, she holds a masters' degree in Training and Development/Technology in Training and a doctorate in Training and Development. Her dissertation research, on communities of practice, fed much of her current interest in social learning and the use of social technologies to support learning in the workplace.

She is the author of *eLearning Solutions on a Shoestring; Better than Bullet Points; From Analysis to Evaluation* and *Social Media for Trainers*, and currently writes the popular "Nuts and Bolts" column for *Learning Solutions Magazine*. She is the recipient of a Training Magazine Editor's Pick Award for instructional design, a NASPE Award for Innovative Government Practice and a North Carolina State University Distinguished Alumni Award.

A popular conference presenter, Dr Bozarth's recent travels have included speaking engagements in Sydney, London, Montreal and Istanbul. Jane and her husband live in Durham, NC, USA.

Blog: http://bozarthzone.blogspot.co.uk
Twitter: @janebozarth

The Really Useful eLearning Instruction Manual. Edited by Rob Hubbard. © 2013 John Wiley & Sons, Ltd.

What's the big idea?

Elearning can take many forms; however, one of the easiest forms to purchase is the self-paced elearning course. Nowadays there are also many authoring tools available that allow you to create learning experiences of your own. So which approach should you take? Well, that depends. This chapter will help you to decide. While we talk here primarily about building "courses", keep in mind that new tools and technologies offer opportunities for developing smaller learning bites, from podcasts and short videos to performance support tools and job aids.

In utilizing elearning for organizational training and development, mistakes are easy – and expensive:

- The company's new training director was hired partly due to his interest in technology-mediated instruction, and he accepted the position partly due to the hiring team's enthusiasm for moving the department into more progressive approaches to delivering training. Based on several surveys and feedback from senior management, the training director contracted for company access to a large vendor catalogue of 1,000 courses on everything from leadership and customer service to LINUX certification. Licences purchased at £50: 2,000. Actual first-year use: 40 people.

- Among the most onerous tasks for the HR department was delivery of basic "orientation" material for new hires, with presenters from different areas offering rote information on benefits and supervising new hires as they filled out forms. The programme was expensive in terms of worker and HR time, required travel for workers outside of the main office, and, because it was only offered once every six weeks, often kept some new hires waiting more than a month to get various personnel paperwork completed. The HR Director compiled all the orientation material and handed it off to a local elearning design firm, who returned a complete online package that new hires could complete any time after hire, with a phone number to contact HR if they had any questions. The programme is not fancy or sophisticated, but employees get the information and the HR department gets the paperwork it needs. The new programme was built on a set of simple templates so that the company's own IT department could make simple changes when forms were updated and benefits information changed. Cost to the organization: £1,000.

- A company requiring mandatory compliance training on sexual harassment contacted many of the vendors offering online courses that met the legal requirements. These were often of good quality and included professionally-produced video scenarios, complex quizzes, and no need for programming, posing minimal technical problems for users and organizations. Additionally, these vendors typically made regular updates to the courses as laws evolved. The best of the products, at £12 per learner, was deemed "too expensive" by management. The company brought in a temporary web developer, who spent six months working full-time to develop an online harassment course. The final product was a text-heavy series of nested web pages with simple clip art that requires learner time of about three hours to complete. Total cost for the temporary web developer and associated expenses? £40,000. Completion rate for this "mandatory" programme? 5%.

Organizations are always looking for effective, efficient ways of enacting work and supporting performance. elearning can answer many economic concerns for an organization: reduction of travel costs for instructors and learners, reduction in costs associated with physical classrooms and paper training materials; reduction in valuable time away from work for training days that often include much "dead time", such as warm-ups, icebreakers, and breaks and lunches that often lag past designated times. Meantime, it provides an effective,[1] timely, convenient, and (if done right) meaningful experience for the learner. But the organization new to elearning is faced with many questions, among them the decision to build content in-house, buy off-the-shelf courses, or outsource custom development work.

Give me the details

The proliferation of "rapid" elearning authoring tools has made actual programming work a much easier task. But it's still work that someone has to do – especially to do it well – and often brings hidden costs. While it's tempting to jump into in-house development, there are a number of factors that come into play and may point toward buying an off-the-shelf product, or outsourcing development work to a vendor. Let's take a look at the reality of elearning development and ways to approach decision-making.

What are you trying to do? For whom?

Too often organizations say, "We need to be online" or "We need to do more training online" without much else in the way of specifics. Questions to consider:

- Do you want to deliver basic overviews of policy and procedure?
- Do you need to deliver an overview of a basic compliance topic – such as safe lifting – to your workforce once per year?
- Do you need complex, detailed simulations for one of your work units?
- Do you need to educate your entire workforce on side effects of a new pharmaceutical currently being developed?
- Are you working with content that is stable or ever-changing, demanding frequent updates and revisions to training programmes?
- Are you looking to reinvent your entire training catalogue?

Factors to consider in decision-making include the amount of proprietary information (information and language specific, or even secret, to the company) and the size of the intended audience: it just doesn't make sense to invest large amounts of staff time in developing bespoke online programmes that will only be used by 25 workers. In the basic buy-v-build decision, Laura Francis offers a quick decision-making tool (see Figure 3.1).

In making decisions, complexity matters, too. Are you interested in distributing content that is essentially only "information"? Really, a simple text-based tutorial reviewing basics of a policy, or a screen capture video walking through, say, entering data into a particular form, isn't very difficult to create and can be highly effective and simple to build yourself. By contrast, building an interactive online course in which learners must work with the data to generate new data, then choose the correct form, then process it through the system, is a much more complex undertaking.

Consider also whether the information is time-critical – is it something that needs to happen quickly? If so, do you have the in-house resources ready, now, to develop that solution? It takes time to learn even simple authoring tools and develop instructional design skills.

Among the options mentioned in the flowchart here are "customize off-the-shelf". Customization can include a simple welcome page outlining specifics of company policy, through to changes in branding elements like corporate colours.

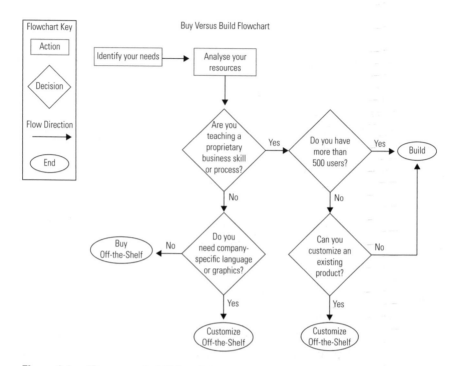

Figure 3.1   *"Buy versus build" flowchart*
© January 2002 from *Learning Circuits* by Laura Francis. Reprinted with permission of the American Society for Training and Development.

If outsourcing is indicated now, use the experience as an opportunity to learn about how the development process works; this can later inform your efforts should you choose to try in-house development later. Consider whether you need a fresh view. Often an outside development team can put a new spin or interesting perspective on a topic that those in-house might be standing too close to see.

What resources do you need?

To develop in-house

At the most basic level: an elearning authoring tool is just that – a tool – and allows someone to build an effective course in the way that word processing software allows them to write a great novel. Talent and skill do matter here. You will need someone with a basic understanding of instructional design and a real command of an authoring tool (in the right hands, even PowerPoint can be used for basic authoring) to develop experiences that support learning and that are not just "presentations". They will also need basic competence working with photos and other graphics. Presumably, you will want to extract usage and test information, and may need someone who knows how to set up your programmes so that data like completions and test scores can be obtained. At a slightly higher level you'll need to consider more advanced instructional design ability, skill in recording/capturing and editing audio, video, and photos, and perhaps skill in working with more sophisticated products such as Adobe Flash and Dreamweaver. Recognize, though, that most smaller companies are resource-constrained and will always have limits when it comes to multimedia production. Note that the *right* talent is important: web developers are not instructional designers, and classroom trainers are not elearning experts. While it's true that building in-house is "cheaper" because money doesn't flow out, in reality it can be very expensive in terms of staff time and can lead to sacrifices to quality. If you are looking to develop what we have usually called "courses", it is possible to build highly effective in-house development teams – but it takes time, the right people and realistic expectations of what they can achieve. Don't feel put off building your own solutions, but be thoughtful about what you want to do and the work it might require. An easy-to-learn tool (good news: tools tend to get better and easier over time) and a grasp of instructional design fundamentals, coupled with clear, realistic objectives, can put in-house development within your reach.

Something smaller?

New tools are making it easier to create what might be called smaller learning experiences. Our learners are increasingly accustomed to identifying and locating their own quick learning solutions. Try asking any adult to describe something they've learned from YouTube; it will be unusual *not* to get an answer. Small bites of learning can be developed and deployed quickly. Consider using approaches such as screencasting, podcasting or uploading video clips by way of short instruction or performance support. Tools vary by price and by learning curve. You don't want something that will take a year to master. Truly, you can build plenty of bad elearning with expensive products. You can likewise build great elearning with inexpensive products and approaches. Again, it's a tool, not a magic wand. For basic programmes don't overlook the capability of PowerPoint or PowerPoint-based tools – but learn to really use them. Get past flying text and meaningless animations, and build effective, engaging narratives and interactions. See J. Bozarth,

Better than Bullet Points: Creating Engaging eLearning with PowerPoint (Wiley, 2013) and the extensive resources provided by Tom Kuhlmann to the Articulate (a PowerPoint-based authoring tool) user community. Also take a look at what's literally in your pocket: smartphones now have excellent photo and video capability, and inexpensive apps can support enhancing and editing photos and video footage. Low-cost and free tools for screencasting, low-cost equipment for recording podcasts, and free or low-cost social tools make creating and publishing content a decidedly less daunting prospect than in the past. In choosing a primary tool or two, try to forecast what you will be doing, mostly. Are you looking at screen recordings of software functions? Videos of complex assembly processes? Do you anticipate highly interactive simulations (really?) or something more like online presentations? Different tools are good for different things, so give thought to the ones that will best serve your anticipated needs.

To buy off-the-shelf

Investing time in choosing the right product, or suite of products, with pricing and contract terms, will provide big payoffs later. Basic resources needed here involve staffing: those who can pinpoint the desired performance outcomes, who have time to review available courses to see whether they support learner achievement of those outcomes, and who understand basic contracting and payment processes and options. Depending on the number of end users, other resources include someone to help with end user support and ongoing communication with the vendor.

To outsource

As with buying off-the-shelf, resources here include people who can help develop a precise picture of what the programme should accomplish, and for whom. Clear communication with the vendor is critical for saving time, money and frustration. The vendor will need to know about the target audience: knowledge levels, experience with the topic and other related training the end users may have had. As for other resources, the vendor can only work with what is provided, and what they produce will be only as good as what they are given: company logos, maps, photos of leaders, any formatting or branding guidelines. High-quality, high-resolution source material (hi-res images of logos and people, for instance) matter, and electronic versions are better than print. If the programme is being moved from an existing classroom version, then the vendor will likely need all the assets from that classroom experience, such as handouts, slide shows, and lesson plans.

For any project you need some basic talent: understanding of instructional design fundamentals, clarity about desired performance, and good project management skills.

So how do I do it?

Building elearning in-house

Approaching in-house development requires careful identification of goals, a clear outline of resources needed and realistic expectations of outcomes:

- Identify needs, performance outcomes, and the target audience.
- Identify means of assessing whether performance objectives have been achieved.
- Develop storyboards and subject them to review by stakeholders, including end users.
- Take inventory: what do you already have? Video cameras, microphones, and in-house voice talent can be very useful tools.
- Identify the best authoring tools for development of the programme(s).
- Assemble assets such as images, sound clips, and case studies or examples.
- Create the programme, ending with recording of any narration or other voiceover.
- Pilot the programme with a portion of the target audience.
- Conduct assessments of the pilot: were objectives achieved?
- Revise, re-evaluate, revise again if necessary.
- Launch: upload for delivery via the Web or the company intranet, notify learners.
- Assess again.

Buying off-the-shelf

Embarking on off-the-shelf purchases can be a dizzying, daunting affair. Before approaching vendors and looking at available products, be sure to get clear on exactly what you are trying to accomplish. That should drive your decision rather than an impressive demo, a catalogue with thousands of courses, or pretty artwork:

- Identify needs, performance outcomes, and the target audience.
- Identify means of assessing whether performance objectives have been achieved.
- Determine whether and what customization will be required: minimal customization or an add-on introduction? Supplemental company-specific information?

- Ask for demonstration periods and some guest accounts, at least a few of which should go to members of the target audience.
- Ensure that content and usability are acceptable for the needs of the organization and stated performance outcomes.
- Negotiate terms: number of seats for what time period? Most vendors will sell per seat, usually for a period of a year. Try to negotiate the purchase of seats available for positions, not people, so that if a person leaves the company a new person can occupy the slot. Be sure pricing includes some support for end users, or at least for the local administrator.
- Make sure agreements include product updates and revisions – in other words, be sure that when you buy the 2013 version you will have access to the 2015 revisions.
- Realize that customization costs extra, and customization beyond insertion of branding elements like logos and company leader photos costs even more. Do you really need the company logo on every screen?

Outsourcing

As with other options, it is critical that you understand goals and anticipated outcomes of the finished product. It is frustrating for both sides to end up at a draft stage to have a stakeholder say, "This isn't what I had in mind", or "This won't solve our problem".

- Identify needs, performance outcomes, and the target audience.
- Identify means of assessing whether performance objectives have been achieved.
- Review sample products from the vendor. Most important: does the vendor's work – finished programmes – achieve the stated desired outcomes? After completing a programme can you do what the course purported to teach you?
- Check references. Were projects completed, on time, per specifications, within budget?
- Clarify: What is the cost of updates and changes? A flat fee per change can be expensive if you only need to swap out the HR Manager's photo every few years. You will want to own the material, and you will want it created in a standard tool so that you can edit it even if your relationship with the vendor ends.
- Remember: data in, data out. The vendor can only work with what they have, so give them everything from logos and company directories to maps and handouts

from any relevant existing classroom programmes. Also, have a conversation about the target audience, covering such things as their skill and knowledge level and their past experience with the course content.

- If outsourcing development, work toward a completed project fee. Per-hour, per-screen, per-learning-minute pricing is rarely a better deal. It's very hard to determine ahead of time how many screens a programme will require or how much time the "average" learner should spend on a programme. Also, realize that intricate simulations and custom graphics and video cost more than text.

Table 3.1   *Checklist for choosing development vendor*

Outsourcing Development: Choosing a Vendor

Process/Project Management

Can the vendor describe the process it uses, step by step? Can the vendor document its own business processes?

What is their particular expertise?

What is their willingness to include you? Will they work from text you wrote, or do they insist on developing everything "their way"?

What is the procedure for managing projects? What mechanisms/people are in place to keep projects on track and on time?

Who is responsible/accountable? Where does the buck stop?

How will the final product be evaluated?

What will you have access to? Can you see storyboards? Or will you have to wait for a prototype?

Deadlines

Will the vendor be available after the product is finished? Do you need him or her to provide training in using the product?

Communication/Access to People

How and when will communication take place? Will you have weekly updates by email? Monthly face-to-face meetings?

Will you be able to meet other people on the team? Are you able to access more than just the sales rep? Can you talk to the designers and programmers?

Does the vendor outsource these services? Where is the designer?

How many people have access to your information?

(Continued)

Table 3.1   *(Continued)*

Contract

Does the vendor offer fixed per-project prices?

Who has ownership of content and products? For what period of time?

Does the contract have a non-performance clause?

If possible, is there also a money-back guarantee?

Do you need security? Will the vendor be dealing with sensitive information?

Is there an allowance for tests/pilots/reasonable changes?

Gut Feeling Issues

When you call, do you get a "live body" or a voicemail? How quickly are calls returned?

Do things seem to be under control or is there always a feeling of chaos?

How long has the vendor been in business? How big is the company?

How was the quality of the proposal? Did they provide the information requested? The vendor
   you choose should be able to follow instructions.

Product

What tools does the vendor use? How flexible is the vendor on this point? (Remember: you want
   a vendor who can create what you need. Do not get talked into changing what you need in
   order to fit the tool the vendor likes.)

Look at samples. Are the products text-heavy? Is there good, meaningful interaction, or just clicking?

Can the vendor produce additional products like support tools, references, and study aids?

From J. Bozarth, *eLearning Solutions on a Shoestring* (San Francisco: Pfeiffer, 2005). Used with permission.

Hints and tips

The best thing you can do: Get educated

The single best thing you can do: get educated. Learn to tell good elearning from bad, and learn enough about development to say: "How did they do that? Can we do that? What would it take to do that?" Google for a topic like "fire extinguisher safety" and see how many text-based and video versions there are on that topic alone. Learn to evaluate them: are they interesting? Do they hold your attention? Too little information? Too much information? What about the tone: cartoony and cute, or serious and dramatic? Which works best with your corporate culture? And most important: at the end, could you use an extinguisher to put out a fire?

Realize that those responsible for budgeting are always looking for corners to cut. It is critical that you understand what you need, at what level of complexity, in order to have the conversations this will require to get the funding you need.

Help your internal team learn to work with and evaluate storyboards. These are meant to be "dummied up" versions of the programme, in sketch-outline form, before expensive or time-consuming elements like audio voiceover and final versions of images are created. Those who do not understand storyboarding often fall into a too-literal analysis of it, leading to long nonproductive discussions on some finer point of a course – like the color of a character's shirt – while failing to accurately assess the whole programme with a more holistic eye. Time spent wisely here will save much time, effort and money later.

Other tips

Think about partnering, not just purchasing. Try to cultivate a friendly relationship with your sales representative that will survive across some years. This can help bring a little extra support, a few favours regarding pricing, and maybe some generosity with payment plans. Bear in mind too that working with a few products, or a few vendors, is easier than managing several different products and agreements. And remember the Golden Rule: treat the vendor as you would want to be treated. Don't ask for quotes on items you really don't intend to buy, don't ask for extraordinary extra work just because you can. The relationship works both ways.

Talk to end users – the learners. This is too often overlooked, or put off until it's too late. Include some learners in needs assessment, basic planning and storyboard reviews – before the project reaches the pilot phase.

Beware of focusing on technology instead of outcomes. The point shouldn't be to build a course, but to solve a problem.

Don't buy anything without some first-hand experience with customer support. Try calling for yourself: does someone answer? Do they know the product? Can they help? The product is only as good as the support.

Even though you may decide to outsource or purchase off-the-shelf content, it's still important to leverage the in-house resources you do have. Will the programme be offered in a blended format, with opportunities for practice provided in the traditional classroom? Can L&D staff help in developing job aids, or engaging learners in online conversations about content via social media tools? Their support for buy-in and transfer are important, too.

When outsourcing, be clear that you will own the final product, and insist that it be created in a non-proprietary authoring tool. You want to be able to access and edit your programmes should the relationship with the vendor end.

The usual suspects

A few caveats.

Vendors selling authoring products unveil dazzling demos created by an army of programmers and graphic artists. Recognize that what you see might be the result of more resources than you will ever have, with staff dedicated completely to mastering the tool.

Realize that in-house training staff feel great ownership for their material and want a hand in moving it to other formats, for example elearning. Work with them to help them feel included and part of the process.

If you don't know what you want, the vendor will make decisions for you. After all, someone has to decide. You need to know your audience, their needs, your performance objectives, your technical requirements and your contracting terms.

Beware of scope creep: adding on this piece and creating another video with another scenario and, oh, let's put a quiz there . . . all lead to project delays. Be clear at the outset what you want to do, and again: utilize the storyboard process to tighten up on the anticipated final design.

Do not ever believe that any tool will overcome a lack of talent and skill. Good elearning is about design, not software.

While it is logical to identify what you want to achieve, for what audience, and by whom, many organizations leap into elearning development by purchasing a tool and then forcing it to fit their situation. This often comes from a seductive vendor pitch or just buying the same product that another company uses. The result: frustrated staff, unfinished or poorly designed programmes, a bad experience for learners, and the final nail: "We tried elearning and it didn't work." Never underestimate the costs of *bad* elearning.

It's a wrap

Remember, those of us in the industry don't want to just build "courses", we want to build learning experiences. And while many can do the former, few are good at the latter. Be honest about your in-house capabilities and, if you find them lacking, either shore them up or look at ways to find quality learning experiences via other means. Good design requires creativity, not just technical expertise. There is no end of bad elearning (or classroom training) available; better decisions here can help to change that.

Note

1. See the "No Significant Difference" site www.nosignificantdifference.org for information on hundreds of studies comparing the effectiveness of online learning to that of the classroom.

Lars Hyland is a respected thought leader and consultant who has been designing award winning learning technology solutions since 1991. Following completion of his postgraduate thesis on the effective design of interactive learning environments, Lars went on to gather experience in all aspects of elearning production and to hold senior management roles within several pioneering elearning companies in the UK.

Lars now advises on learning technology strategy and best practice for a wide range of public and private sector organizations, in the UK and internationally. Lars has spoken at major conferences around the world and co-authored the 2006 DTI Global Watch Mission Report, "Beyond eLearning". He is currently Head of Consulting Services at Epic Learning Group and is also Founder of Retenda.com, an innovative online service that dramatically improves learning transfer for corporate training and education.

LinkedIn: http://www.linkedin.com/in/larshyland
Twitter: @larshyland

The Really Useful eLearning Instruction Manual. Edited by Rob Hubbard. © 2013 John Wiley & Sons, Ltd.

What's the big idea?

If you've ever felt daunted by the prospect of creating and deploying an elearning solution, then don't worry – most people feel that way, including the professionals who do it day in day out. The reason is that every project has unique aspects to it, some of which you can control, some of which you can only influence or respond to. So the first and last thing you should take away from this chapter is this – don't panic, keep calm, communicate clearly, stay open to change, back up regularly and not only will you enjoy the ride, you'll deliver a learning experience that you, your team and learners will value.

Methodologies – horses for (elearning) courses

There are many formal project management methodologies that are aimed at helping you deliver projects successfully. You may have come across software design terms such as Waterfall, PRINCE2, Agile, Extreme – all of which attempt to guide you through the wide variety of conditions and complexity of projects you may face. These have influenced the field of instructional design, in particular the commonly adopted ADDIE (Analyze, Design, Develop, Implement and Evaluate) Model, but viewed generically, they can be broadly categorized as either being incremental, phased or iterative in style.

An Incremental method tends to follow a linear step-by-step route through a series of activities to reach a formal deliverable. An Iterative approach favours smaller, frequent cycles of production that generate early results but with the expectation that these will be constantly refined and added to. Indeed iterative processes can extend beyond delivery to your learners so that you are in effect in "perpetual beta" and never consider your elearning product as final. A Phased approach meets Incremental and Iterative methods in the middle, essentially allowing you to have more structure to your project with defined deliverables but with the option to work on some activities in parallel, as well as have planned additional cycles of production that add functionality and further content beyond the date of initial delivery.

For those working in large organizations you may find that a certain methodology is imposed upon you as policy. For those in small organizations, working individually or as part of a virtual team, you may have no constraints or structure. Neither blindly following methodology nor making it up as you go along are good strategies for success. Both these extremes can lead to certain death for your project if you do not remain vigilant.

You can find plenty of online resources and books that cover the details of these project management methodologies. What we will concentrate on here is how to draw on the good practice that these embody and adapt them to meet the particular and varied needs of elearning production. Before we dive into the detail, let's recognize some key principles and approaches that underpin any successful technical development and content rich production process which will help you deliver reliably, robustly and in a timely and cost efficient way.

Give me the details

Before you start, make sure you answer the questions in the following table.

Table 4.1 *Preparing for your elearning project*

What are you building and why?	Check that elearning is the right solution to the problem you are addressing.
What are your constraints?	Time, budget, technical environment, production values.
How does it break down?	Identify the different activities/components within your learning solution and adapt your development approach to suit each component's relative complexity.
Who's doing what?	Secure the right skills and manage your team.
What tools and systems are you using?	Be aware of their strengths and weaknesses, backing up.
How are you communicating?	With your team, your stakeholders, your learners.
What happens after you deliver?	Update and maintenance, transfer and ongoing support.

What are you building and why?

As it stands elearning still has no real commonly agreed definition and can encompass a wide range of digital content types. Your palette is wide and can include the following:

Table 4.2 *Digital learning content asset types*

Interactive tutorials	Tutorials are most people's experience of structured elearning which are typically anywhere between 10 and 60 minutes' study time (anything more and you should create another module).
Simulations	More immersive scenario-led learning that may include complex branching functionality.
Video and audio	Media clips that can be simple recordings of experts, structured interviews or full dramatized sequences.
Online presentations/ webinars	Real-time online events with slides or recordings made accessible post delivery.
Job aids/reference documentation	PDF and other digital files that can be accessed online.
Mobile apps	These can include any or all of the other types listed here but there are specific considerations where the app runs natively on a specific mobile device such as a smartphone or tablet. For example, to integrate with available functions such as a camera, location and other sensors. Additionally where a "responsive design" may be needed so that the app resizes and reconfigures for different screen sizes.
Collaborative activities	Online exercises that bring virtual groups of learners together using tools such as discussion forums, social media and collaborative document creation tools.
Games/data-driven modelling	Can incorporate more bespoke functionality that is data driven, simulating more complex situations and scenarios. This also draws on proven gaming dynamics that drive motivation and engagement such as levelling-up, achievements/ badges, and social integration to share activity and collaborate with others. More in-depth tracking of learner behaviour can inform the impact of both the current and future solution designs.

Now, while elearning is increasingly likely to play a role in most learning solutions going forward, it's important to check that the project is best served in this way. Being clear about the type of learning being covered will help guide the recommended blend of content to be created. For example:

- Would performance support or a change to current working practices be a better solution than training staff in working methods that may benefit from simplification?
- Is the target audience culturally ready to learn in this way? Can they more readily get together and learn face-to-face in small groups without formal support?
- Is the technical environment available sufficient to allow a well-designed elearning experience to take place?
- Are you clear about the performance/productivity measures you will use to determine the impact of the elearning?

Challenging your brief early on is important and will ensure that you focus on projects that will make a real difference.

What are your constraints?

You need to be very clear about the parameters you are working within for each project you undertake as this will heavily influence the design and production decisions you make. Available time is the most common constraint of training projects. Too often the training requirements of a wider change programme are considered very late in the process and so you'll need to respond quickly within a limited available window – this may be a matter of days, weeks or months depending on the scale of change being implemented. There is little real value in building a fantastic, yet complex elearning experience if it can't be delivered in time and will be too time-consuming to maintain. Similarly, there is little value in producing very simple, unchallenging learning that makes no impact on your audience. Getting the balance right within the development time window you have is crucial so that you can deliver on time with minimal risk of slippage.

Likewise, you will invariably have a defined budget available to spend on internal and external resources for your project. This will clearly affect the production values you can incorporate into your solution. Now, not all projects need or will benefit from a "Rolls-Royce" treatment. What's more important is a strong conceptual design that will impact your audience, irrespective of the production values you then apply. It is also worth considering the maxim "less is more" – targeting your budget on what matters most, rather than spreading yourself thin to deliver more content but in a uniformly uninspiring format.

In many large organizations you will come across legacy IT infrastructure. It is still not uncommon to see early browsers such as Internet Explorer 5.5, Windows NT operating systems as well as congested networks that limit the available bandwidth. You may also have to contend with virtualized desktop environments such as Citrix which can also restrict what can be implemented.

Increasingly you will need to consider mobile devices as these are formally (or informally) introduced into the workplace. These can add further complexity (for example, Apple devices at the time of writing do not support Flash) in ensuring your learning can be accessed by your intended target audience. This consideration extends also to how your learners will *find and launch* the elearning you offer. This can be a frustrating process for the learner depending on the Learning Management System (LMS) in use, unless carefully managed.

An additional consideration is any accessibility requirements to ensure all learners, including those with vision, hearing or other impairment, can interact and receive the desired learning experience. This may mean some interactive treatments need to be avoided during the design process (such as drag and drop exercises). There may also be a need to develop additional versions of your elearning content or provide added functionality such as support for screen-reader software.

How does it break down?

Designing a full learning experience is likely to include more than one large monolithic elearning module. It is important to think beyond the single course completed in one sitting, and instead think more in terms of a campaign of activities that collectively will have more lasting impact on the learner. These activities will be a mix of components, some functionally complex, others simple documents. Each of these deliverables does not necessarily need to follow the same uniform production process. Doing so may introduce unwelcome overhead and cost you time and money. A simulation module may require more in-depth design and bespoke technical production compared to a simple tutorial that can be produced in a standard rapid authoring tool. Equally, producing a video for inclusion within an elearning module is in itself a project with its own specific production process. Managing these strands takes careful orchestration so that each element is ready to be integrated into the whole at the right moment.

Who's doing what?

As we can see, elearning production requires a mix of technical, creative, instructional and administrative skills. The various roles are shown in the table below:

Table 4.3 *Common elearning production roles*

Project Manager	Coordinates all production activities and communicates with stakeholders, provides regular progress reporting against plan (time and budget).
Learning Designer	Ensures learning objectives are clear and designs a content treatment that is instructionally sound.
Interactive Designer	Designs usable, navigable interactions that deliver the learning content treatment.
Scriptwriter/ Storyboarder	Screen by screen blueprint of all words, images and other assets that will make up the final elearning deliverable.
Graphic Designer	Visual treatment of overall look and feel and navigation, as well as production of individual content images and animations.
Author	Implements the approved detailed storyboard, using supplied graphics and any other media assets in an elearning development tool. These tools usually offer efficient ways to create commonly used interactivity.
Programmer	Builds functionality that cannot be created using standard tools. Advises on any technical issues that can affect successful delivery such as LMS tracking (for example, SCORM) and the specific IT environment of the target audience.
Tester/Quality Assurance Reviewer	Systematic checking of all documentation, scripts, storyboards, prototypes and working versions to ensure that content is accurate and functionality works as intended.

Depending on the circumstances and the nature of your project, you will need different numbers of people to fulfil these roles. For small projects, based on standard off-the-shelf authoring tools, it is possible for one person to take on nearly all these roles. However it is rare that one person can be expert in all areas. Indeed, the reason so much "rapid elearning" is not as good as it could be is that there is a severe deficiency in one or more of these competencies. In most professional elearning companies, different people specialize in each of these areas and can generally offer higher levels of productivity and skill as a result.

As the team size grows and the number of stakeholders widens, the importance of regular and more formal communication increases. As the project manager, there needs to be regular reporting, charting progress through each stage of production. It's advisable to use a scheduling tool such as Microsoft Project to detail all tasks and activities and to allocate resources accordingly within your team and stakeholder group. Undoubtedly dates will move around and a tool of this sort can save you much time and energy. Better still, you can use online collaborative project management tools such as Basecamp or Huddle that will help keep documentation and communication in one shared space.

If your production team does not physically sit close to each other, then a vital line of informal communication can be lost. For example, ensuring that a graphic designer interprets the descriptions within the storyboard/script can be accomplished by quick conversations and looks over the shoulder. This works wonders in minimizing rework. This can also now be easily achieved virtually through collaborative screen sharing and unified messaging platforms such as Microsoft Lync and Google Hangouts.

The collaborative nature of the production process can be deepened to include your subject-matter experts and stakeholders by using a collaborative elearning authoring environment. These tools sit in the Cloud, on the internet, into which your team can share work in progress with stakeholders at the appropriate moment.

So how do I do it?

A typical elearning production process

The most common professional model used in elearning production is based upon a structured Incremental/Phased approach. At its heart, this typically maps to the generic ADDIE methodology, the steps being:

- Analysis
- Design
- Development
- Implementation or Delivery
- Evaluation.

You'll find most specialist development teams have evolved this into a production process that will usually include the following key steps:

- Gathering Requirements
- High Level Design Specification
    - Learning Design
    - Visual Design
    - Technical Specification
- Prototype/Walkthrough/User Testing
- Storyboard/Interactive Script
- Asset Production
    - Graphics and animation
    - Audio
    - Video
- Programming/Authoring
- Testing (alpha, beta, gold)
- Final Delivery
- Deployment
- Review/Evaluation.

At all key stages there are review points to allow subject-matter experts and stake-holders (including users themselves) to comment and changes to be made before giving formal approval to proceed on through the project. This is invaluable in maintaining control of your project as the further you move through the production process, the more significant the impact which requests to change earlier design decisions can have on timelines and costs. However, it can also mean you may not be able to respond as readily to external changes or new information which would lead to an improved design solution.

The following table shows some hints and tips you would do well to take on board when working through each of these stages.

However, there are times, perhaps increasingly, where these strategies are not enough. For example, the content requirements underpinning your design may be under continual change right up to and beyond your nominal launch date; or the ways in which your users prefer to access their learning may be evolving rapidly which makes it difficult for you to make fixed technical assumptions.

An Agile approach

Where this is the case, an alternative approach is available which will require you to accept different principles and ways of working in order to deliver faster more frequent deliverables that iteratively improve over time. This Agile Model is based on valuing:[1]

- individuals and interactions over processes and tools
- working software over comprehensive documentation
- customer collaboration over contract negotiation
- responding to change over following a plan.

You can see how the principles and ideals behind the Agile Manifesto can, if genuinely adopted by all stakeholders, radically re-shape the dynamics of the elearning development process:

- Our highest priority is to satisfy the customer through early and continuous delivery of valuable software.
- Welcome changing requirements, even late in development. Agile processes harness change for the customer's competitive advantage.
- Deliver working software frequently, from a couple of weeks to a couple of months, with a preference for the shorter timescale.
- Business people and developers must work together daily throughout the project.
- Build projects around motivated individuals.
- Give them the environment and support they need, and trust them to get the job done.
- The most efficient and effective method of conveying information to and within a development team is face-to-face conversation.
- Working software is the primary measure of progress.

Table 4.4 *A typical elearning production process*

Gathering Requirements	The more information you can capture at the outset the more likely you will produce a learning solution that delivers real value. So document the following:
	– The business objective underpinning this learning solution
	– The measures of success by which this project will be evaluated
	– How this elearning integrates within a wider learning/change programme
	– The roles, responsibilities and expected time commitment required of all stakeholders, subject-matter experts and the production team
	– The characteristics and needs of your target audience (job roles, working environment, prior elearning experience, organizational culture and tone of voice, line management support)
	– The milestone dates for deployment
	– The internal and external budget assigned to support the project.
	REVIEW/APPROVAL POINT
High Level Design Specification	The design specification can now be shaped to meet the requirements gathered. The three key dimensions of learning design, visual design and technical specification intertwine and influence each other in defining the final solution you arrive at.
	Learning Design
	– Detail all content and learning objectives to be covered, together with expectations on where and who will provide source material and subject matter expertise. This should include interviews/contributions with key stakeholders and representatives of your target audience. Don't just take your sponsor's word for it.
	Visual Design
	– Consider any existing branding guidelines
	– Determine a style of treatment that best suits the learning content (e.g. photographic, illustrative, metaphorical, abstract)
	– Bear in mind any technical constraints to ensure the visual design is actually workable.

Technical Specification

- Capture the minimum specifications of PC/laptop/mobile devices which should include the operating system, screen resolutions and browser versions to be supported and availability of other required software (for example, Flash)
- Clarify the network bandwidth available and policy for the use of rich media such as video and audio
- Detail any tracking requirements of an available SCORM compliant LMS or other system for recording user activity
- Clarify the preferred implementation method for any accessibility requirements
- Always conduct a common sense check with your target audience – what is it actually like to access current elearning?

REVIEW/APPROVAL POINT

Prototype/ Walkthrough/ User Testing	This is an early opportunity to test and confirm the design decisions you have made. Depending on the development tools used and the nature of the project, this can either be a paper exercise, a fully interactive section of content, or a rough rendering of some specific interaction or functionality. In both cases it is important that all stakeholders, user representatives and the production team now have a common understanding of the design so there are no surprises going forward.
Storyboard/ Interactive Script	With all the key design decisions confirmed, full and explicit treatment of all content is scripted. This will include:

- All text on screen
- Descriptions of graphics required
- Audio and video scripts
- Navigational and interaction instructions for the author/programmer
- Links to reference material/files that will be included within the elearning module.

There are some additional considerations to include that will help you keep the project on track and be maintainable in the future.

- Settle on a consistent file-naming schema for all digital assets that will be created. This will include section numbering, image files, video, audio and where applicable animation files. Remember to leave gaps in your number sequences (for example, number things as multiples of 5 or 10) to allow for any future insertions of additional content)
- Be clear about the interactive treatment expected at each stage. This may be a numbered template name and short description (for example, Multiple Choice Question with 3 options, 1 correct answer). This will be a direct link to the interactions defined within the Design Specification.
- Version control the script documents so you have a record of change and can easily revert to previous releases should this be necessary. |

(Continued)

Table 4.4 *(Continued)*

	REVIEW/APPROVAL POINT
Asset Production	Depending on the media mix of your design, then once you have an approved script/storyboard, you can begin creating/sourcing the assets ready for subsequent authoring. **Graphics** – try and create or source your images in the highest resolution possible. This will give you more options later where images may be re-used outside of the elearning module (say for a printed poster). It will also mean that you can more easily support higher resolution devices as they come along. For example, image files developed for an early Apple iPad will not look as good on an iPad with a higher resolution Retina display. Equally, a module designed for a certain screen size and form factor may not look as good when used on a larger screen size with a higher resolution. With such a plethora of devices, there is an increasing requirement to be able to support multiple environments which may mean that your elearning needs to be responsive and offer alternative assets (for example, a smaller sized video) where required to optimize the experience for the user. For example, the same module may re-size itself automatically for a user on a smartphone (using smaller image files), on a tablet (using higher resolution files) and dynamically on a PC/laptop browser where the user can change the window size themselves. **Video** – Create the video in the highest possible resolution (HD format for example) so that you can generate multiple versions to suit the available screen size and network bandwidth available. Depending on the video player you are using, you will be able to dynamically switch to the appropriate file format. You may also need to consider how the video is shot to ensure that the learner can engage with it as intended. A video viewed on a small smartphone may not enable a user to determine much detail so make sure that this does not compromise the learning experience. **Audio** – Use a good quality microphone at all times and capture at the highest available level – your learners will thank you, as there is nothing more tiring than to try and discern what is being said against unnecessary background noise. Ideally, you will be able to process/edit the audio to remove any anomalies and to keep audio files as small as possible. Use the best available encoding format you can. **Animation** – To date, Flash has been the tool of choice for creating animation and movement within elearning and the web as a whole. However, the increased adoption of HTML5 is providing a more flexible (although not yet as functional) framework with which to support multiple devices, in particular Apple iOS where Flash is not available. Animated sequences which are largely non-interactive can be made into video files for easier deployment.

Programming/ Authoring

This is where you bring all your content and assets together and breathe interactive life into our elearning. The choice of tool you use will affect the range of interactions you can readily use and you will have defined these in the Design Specification so that all stakeholders are aligned in their expectations.

Where you are using an off-the-shelf tool – Lectora, Articulate, Captivate to name a few of the most popular – then you will be able to map your design to available functionality. If you have more technical skills available then in some cases these can be customised beyond what is provided out of the box.

When working with an external elearning specialist, they may use their own proprietary tools which can typically be extended to incorporate unique interactions and functionality where required.

Increasingly, there are tools available which enable you to manage the whole authoring and publication process online (for example, Epic's GoMo Learning and BrainShark). These allow you to collaboratively author with a geographically spread team and deploy to multiple devices as required.

Testing

There are so many different elements that must come together in an elearning module it is imperative that you plan for comprehensive testing. The key areas you must focus on are:

– adherence to the approved script/storyboard and checking that no spelling or factual errors have arisen during the production process (especially within images)

– assets are in the right format and resolution and perform as expected in the destination user environment

– layout of text and assets onscreen are as expected (tested in a variety of environments if you have a responsive design that adapts to suit the device of the user)

– links to external assets/resources all work successfully, accessibility functions work as expected

– tracking functions (SCORM or otherwise) perform as expected including pass marks, randomization/pooling of assessment questions

– navigation and branching logic all works as intended.

In addition, early and regular user testing is advised as this can highlight problems of understanding and potential confusion created by content and interactivity that otherwise works as intended. Pay particular attention to the phrasing of questions and their options, and any bespoke functionality that strays away from user expectations.

(Continued)

Table 4.4 *(Continued)*

A hangover from traditional software development is the terminology "alpha", "beta" and "gold".

Alpha refers to the first full version of the module that your stakeholders are invited to test and review. There is an expectation that there will be some errors and functional bugs to correct but it should, if earlier testing has been conducted, by and large, be a working version.

Feedback from stakeholders and user representatives is collected – ideally using an online tool that helps you filter and manage the workflow of changes – and corrections and fixes are made.

The beta version has incorporated all the identified and agreed changes and is reviewed by stakeholders to confirm that it represents the final version. There should only be a very few minor changes at this point before you can declare the module as the final bold version. "Gold" harks back to the days when final deliverables were issued on CD-ROMs. It is more common that files are issued digitally and online, although a safety copy on DVD (or other physical storage format) would be advisable.

REVIEW/APPROVAL POINT

Final Delivery	Final deployment of your elearning may require sending to a staging server for formal testing prior to it being made available live to users. This is usually the process when the elearning is made available via an LMS or other tracking system.
	Your work does not stop here, however. Your target audience needs to know the learning is available and so appropriate communication needs to be issued if not already scheduled within a wider change management programme. Usage reports should then be monitored to check that no problems arise which need prompt attention.
	When you have stakeholders taking more direct responsibility for their target audience then provision of support documentation and guidelines will help them become self-sufficient more quickly.
	Post completion of your elearning module there should be available support to aid transfer of the learning into action in the workplace. This can take the form of action-oriented reminders to combat forgetting, using tools like Retenda and goal-based learning systems such as Goalgetter.
Review/ Evaluation	Once final approval has been received, it is good practice to schedule a review meeting to capture any learning gained through the production process so you can make improvements for the future.
	At the appropriate time, evaluation of the elearning against the original business and learning objectives will ensure you measure the impact made. This may be confounded with any number of other concurrent changes experienced by your target audience but you can usually demonstrate what difference the learning has made to performance and productivity, as long as you have focused on the right measures in the first place.

- Agile processes promote sustainable development. The sponsors, developers and users should be able to maintain a constant pace indefinitely.
- Continuous attention to technical excellence and good design enhances agility.
- Simplicity – the art of maximizing the amount of work not done – is essential.
- The best architectures, requirements and designs emerge from self-organizing teams.
- At regular intervals, the team reflects on how to become more effective, then tunes and adjusts its behaviour accordingly.

With this in place, a working elearning module can be sprint-built in a matter of days or weeks (typically a four-week cycle) and then feedback is gathered from users for implementation in a subsequent build cycle. This appears to compare favourably with the more structured process which typically can take 8–12 weeks or longer before a deliverable is available.

Establishing these principles can clash with prevailing organizational culture but when successfully in place there can be a real step change in productivity. Learners can receive more frequent, focused learning support that feels timely, relevant and refreshingly clear. Now this is still possible to achieve with the more structured ADDIE approach too, especially if the adapted strategies above are in place. So it is important to understand from the outset the dynamics of the project you are embarking upon and select the development process best suited to it.

Hints and tips

Rapid elearning production can, if you are not careful, be a euphemism for "rushed and not thought through". If this is the case, you will launch elearning that will have little positive impact. However, we do live in a world of increasing pace, where change is occurring much more quickly, demanding shorter production cycles. This does not necessarily mean you should bypass the best practices listed above, but instead find more efficient ways to complete each key stage in less time.

Here are some useful strategies for achieving a faster, smoother production process:

- Contracting with subject-matter experts and stakeholders to agree that their responsibility is solely to identify and provide accurate source content, and the production team delivers the learning design in a manner that in their expert opinion best delivers the learning objectives and meets the needs of the target audience.

- Agree that any content that cannot be sourced in a timely manner is excluded from the current learning programme, or treated as a simple reference document that can be included much later in the current production cycle. Too often too much content is asked for within a learning design which can cloud the actual key messages. It is almost always far better to ruthlessly remove anything that gets in the way of delivering your primary objectives loud and clear.
- Use Action Mapping techniques to focus your learning design on the actions learners need to take to effect the change in behaviour required that will deliver the business objective. It's about performance, not information giving.
- Use tools that have already been proved to work reliably within your technical environment.
- Reduce review time windows to a single day and agree to meet (physically or virtually) to conduct the review process together in real time, recording any change requests as you go and agreeing approval in principle at the end of the session. Having an agreed meeting date that is diarized and prioritized above normal business activity (tricky to achieve but worth trying) will ensure there are no bottlenecks.

The usual suspects

While we have looked at how to do things right, it always pays dividends to recognize how things can go wrong. The table below shows some common pitfalls for you to avoid with some resolution strategies.

Table 4.5 *Common pitfalls and resolution strategies*

A solution looking for a problem	elearning (or any training for that matter) is useless if it is not solving a real problem for your target audience. Check with and challenge your stakeholders that there is real demand and support for a learning solution.
Everything and the kitchen sink, please	Just because there are no real physical space constraints doesn't mean that your elearning should contain all possible content. Subject-matter experts too often find it difficult to concentrate on the key learning points that learners new to the subject must grasp. Repeatedly challenge whether requested content is really necessary and keep your core messages clear and uncluttered. Use the "Campaign not Course" thinking to restructure the components and activities of your overall learning solution so it remains understandable and actionable.

Time, budget and quality expectations unbalanced	It's crucial that all stakeholders have a realistic understanding of what it is possible to achieve within the available time, budget and resource constraints. Using step-by-step task planning reveals the true nature of commitment required to source, review and approve content, the lead-time for producing video sequences and bespoke interactivity. Often, less is more, so reducing the quantity of material to be produced and using the freed time and budget to deliver a higher quality experience will most likely have a more positive impact on your target audience.
Incoherent and inappropriate review feedback	Be clear with stakeholders as to their role and the nature of feedback you are looking for at each stage of production. It helps no one if there is not a shared vision in place from the outset as you will continue to receive feedback that fails to constructively push the project forward and instead undermines progress. Where you have large numbers of stakeholders, use tools that standardize the collection of comments and automatically link it to relevant pages/screens thus reducing duplication of effort and ambiguity.
Failure to track production time spent	Most specialist elearning production companies use time management tools to track how much time is spent on each part of the production process. This is a good discipline for internal teams too even if there is no formal obligation to do so. It helps you evidence the real time taken to implement each task, to assess the relative efficiency and effectiveness of your team, and to budget accordingly and learn for future projects.
Check and test your technical environment	Plan in an early technical prototype that ensures you have proven to your own satisfaction that when you deliver the final solution, it really will work within the environment you planned for. It's no comfort to find out at the point of delivery that the "approved" technical specification was not quite accurate and your elearning will not work within the real available bandwidth, or won't actually track with the LMS. Note that this can also have positive outcomes in that legacy constraints (such as old internet browsers) may not actually need to be supported, giving you more freedom to use modern design techniques.
Budget for change	Always ensure there is both time and budget available within your project planning to deal with unexpected change. It is much easier for all concerned to work with a 10–15% buffer that will give you some room to respond to requests/issues/obstacles without having to go back to project sponsors for additional time/budget just before delivery. Ideally, you should look beyond final delivery to a subsequent updated version that can take into account post-launch feedback.

(Continued)

Table 4.5 *(Continued)*

Forgetting to evaluate post implementation	The real success of your project is not delivering on time and to budget – that is just the beginning. Has the solution had the desired impact? Have you measures in place to capture this evidence? A positive change to individual and organizational performance will do more to secure you a regular stream of projects than a portfolio of nice-looking yet underused elearning modules that have made no real impact on your audience.
Failing to consider the WHOLE user experience	You may deliver a fantastic learning design, yet if your users cannot easily find it on the corporate system, or their line managers refuse them the time to complete the training, then you will not have succeeded. There are a host of factors that go beyond the design and implementation of the elearning itself. While you have less control over these, it is important to address them openly with the relevant stakeholders and monitor them closely. There are often simple solutions that can be put in place, or an adjustment to your design approach can be made which will navigate around an issue that would limit its impact.

This list is by no means exhaustive. There are plenty more issues out there, so it's important to remain vigilant and flexible at all times.

It's a wrap

As you can see there are many things to consider throughout the elearning production process. But as stated at the outset, above all else remember this – don't panic, keep calm, communicate clearly, stay open to change, back up regularly and not only will you enjoy the ride, you'll deliver a learning experience that you, your team and learners will value.

Note

1. Agile Alliance (2001). Manifesto for Agile Software Development from http://www.agilemanifesto.org/1111.

5. Making the Most of Memory

Rob Hubbard ·

Rob Hubbard is a designer through and through and is fascinated by how we learn, what we remember and why we pay attention to certain things. He most enjoys designing learning solutions; including elearning strategies, learning systems, apps, scenarios and online courses. He is a huge enthusiast of all that technology can offer to enhance learning and abhors bad design in any form.

In 2005, Rob founded LearningAge Solutions, which has grown to become a leading digital learning company in the UK. He has led numerous projects with many premier global organizations, gaining recognition with a number of awards. He has been involved in the eLearning Network for many years, serving on the Board for four years and as the elected Chair for two. He regularly speaks at conferences, blogs and judges awards.

Blog: http://robhubbard.wordpress.com
LinkedIn: robhubbard16
Twitter: @robhubbard

What's the big idea?

Memory is the foundation of knowledge. Without memory we would start each day afresh and have to relearn everything we need to know to survive. More than that, our memories of where we've been and what we've done make us who we are.

Memory is amazing. We are able to transport ourselves back in time to a moment and experience it again. This includes not just images but sounds, smells and feelings. Our ability to time travel in this way is magical and this is probably why we tend to think that our memories are both accurate and infallible.

But just how truthful is memory and how easy is it to retain and recall knowledge and experiences reliably?

- Think of the last piece of training you undertook, whether in a classroom or online. As a percentage, how much of it can you currently remember?
- Now think back to a significant moment in your life. It could be your first kiss, the birth of a child or achieving a long-term goal. How well do you recall that moment?

The odds are that you remember little of your last training experience and seemingly a great deal about the significant moment in your life. Some memories require effortful processing – we need to work hard to remember them. Others we seem to commit to memory very easily with automatic processing. Unfortunately the majority of what we need to learn to do our jobs falls into the former category.

If any of us stop to think about it, it's obvious that we forget things at an alarming rate. Why then should we expect those participating in our training programmes to go through them once and then retain that information forever?

In this short chapter I don't want to spend long covering what we know about the mechanics of memory. Reading John Medina's book *Brain Rules*[1] will give you a good grounding in current thinking. Rather I'll give you a quick summary of how memory works and focus on practical approaches you can take to make the most of it – this is a Really Useful Instruction Manual after all.

Give me the details

The truth of the matter is that we know very little about how
memory works. The way that we form, store, access and forget
memories is hugely complex. There are a lot of long-held beliefs
about memory that turn out to be wrong, so it's time to do a little myth-busting. Best
put your safety goggles on – sparks might fly.

Myth #1: Once we commit something to memory it remains there unchanged forever

Allow me to introduce you to Hermann Ebbinghaus, the increasingly quoted pio-
neer in memory research. Ebbinghaus conducted experiments on himself over 30
years from 1879, testing his ability to recall nonsense words. He found that people
forget 90% of what they learn in the classroom after 30 days and that the majority of
forgetting occurs in the first few hours.

You might like to read that last sentence again.

This finding makes a mockery of traditional teaching methods, and I'm including
any one-hit training intervention here, whether in the classroom or online. His
studies may have been conducted over one hundred years ago; however, they have
been reproduced in numerous more recent studies. It is ironic that his work on
memory was forgotten for so long.

Ebbinghaus was the first to identify that how well we commit something to memory
depends on the extent that we pay attention to it. Let's tackle this first.

Your attention please

The human brain can hold somewhere between three to five pieces of information
at a time for less than 30 seconds. What happens in these initial few seconds has
a huge impact on how the information is stored and whether we will be able to
retrieve it.

Further, as humans we pay attention to some things more than others and it all
comes back to animal instincts and evolution. We've only been walking upright as

a race for a heartbeat in evolutionary terms and the things we pay most attention to are:

- Can it hurt me?
- Can I eat it?
- Can I mate with it?

Also referred to as the "Three Fs" – fight, food and (ahem) procreate. We have special parts of our brains devoted to these concepts. Advertising plays on this and the most successful adverts engage one or more of these concepts.

How many training experiences tick one of these boxes? Not many, that's for sure. So we need to find other ways to help people remember things.

Myth #2: Memory is like a library of video recordings

A common misconception is that we accurately record experiences using our senses and then store these memories sequentially in one place within our brains, a bit like pressing record on a video recorder then placing the tape on a shelf.

Think again. Instead, you store different sensory elements of an experience in different parts of your brain. John Medina describes it like a blender running with the lid off, slicing and dicing the experience and spraying fragments over our mind. Further, memories are not static; they migrate around different areas of the brain over time.

When we recall the memory, the brain reassembles these fragments. However, it remixes them *with regard to our current situation*. It reassembles the fragments in ways that pander to our ego and paint us in the best possible light. In this way, our current situation colours our memories and this is why eye-witness accounts are so unreliable. Indeed, it is possible without too much effort to implant vivid "memories" in peoples' minds.

Kim Wade[2] at the University of Warwick demonstrated this when she colluded with the parents of her student subjects to mess with their heads. She doctored old family photographs to show them having experiences that never actually took place – in this case a hot air balloon ride. Two weeks after the students were shown the modified photographs, half of the participants had "memories" of the fictional hot air balloon ride that never took place.

Interestingly, the sensory information stored from an experience is generally pretty accurate; it's in the reassembly of this information into memory where the brain shows a sycophantic artistic licence.

So how do I do it?

Although we have a limited understanding of how memory works and how people learn, there are a few methods that we know can make something more memorable. Employing them in the design of your learning interventions will help people to retain knowledge and put their learning into practice.

Teach the bare minimum

First of all identify which elements, if anything, of the material, people actually need to be able to recall *instantly, without any support*. The amount of knowledge we need to hold in our heads to do our jobs is decreasing and this trend looks set to continue. The simple fact is that we are typically never more than a few centimetres away from a device that we can use to access vast amounts of information, whether it's a PC, tablet or mobile phone. This is a good thing since our jobs are more complex than ever.

The most common mistake in training is to bombard learners with everything that we think might be useful for them to know about a particular subject. Clive Shepherd describes this as like "trying to drink from a fire hose". The assumption here is that peoples' brains are but empty vessels into which we can pour whatever quantity of knowledge we want. If they don't remember it all, then they're either a bit thick or they haven't been paying enough attention. I come across this belief with worrying frequency and sometimes from people who really should know better.

Given what we now know about how limited our attention is and how hard it is to remember things, it is crucial to focus people's efforts on helping them to remember the vital key facts or concepts. You are probably thinking "OK that makes sense. But how can I identify what people really need to know?"

A first step would be following Cathy Moore's Action Mapping process.[3] This design process has gathered momentum over the last five years to such an extent that it's one of the most widely used design methodologies, in the UK at least. Action

Mapping won't fit every project; however it's an excellent starting point. You'll find Action Mapping referenced throughout this book and whilst a number of us have been using similar approaches for years, Cathy was the first person to nail it into such a robust and reliable process.

In brief, here is how the process works:

1. First, identify the business or organizational objective that you are trying to achieve.
2. Next, identify all the *real world* actions that people need to take to achieve that organizational goal.
3. Thirdly, design ways for people to practise these real world actions in as realistic a way as possible.
4. Then (and this is what I love most about Action Mapping), identify the minimum information that people need if they are to complete these practice activities.

Finally, look carefully at this information. Identify what you'll need people to be able to hold in their heads and call to mind instantly – what they need to know, and what they just need an awareness of, so they can find it when they need it.

Encourage repetition

We know from research as early as that of Ebbinghaus that repetition works, so cover key facts and concepts multiple times throughout the learning intervention and beyond. There is debate on whether the intervals between the repetitions should increase or be equal. In Jeffrey Karpicke and Henry Roediger's small study in 2007,[4] they found that increasing the intervals between repetitions was more effective for short-term memory, whereas equal spacing of repetition was more effective at enhancing long-term memory, especially when feedback was given to correct errors. One thing is for sure; repeating key facts at intervals increases the likelihood of people remembering them.

A simple way to achieve this is through a knowledge test quiz with informative feedback. The quiz itself becomes the form of repetition. Numerous low-cost quiz-building systems exist that can be used for this. I recommend creating a question bank from which a smaller sub-set of questions can be randomly pulled, so the quiz can be used repeatedly at intervals after the initial training intervention.

You can also repeat a concept or fact by building upon it during the learning intervention, for example "So we've seen how . . . To build on that . . .". This should make the repetition less obvious, while retaining the flow of the learning process.

One of the best ways of encouraging repetition is through a fun, game-like experience. When playing, gamers repeat the same actions again and again and again; seeing what works and what doesn't, adjusting their approach and improving their performance. If their engagement level is high, they do this without thinking. This is one of the reasons I believe game-based learning shows such promise for teaching and learning purposes.

Consider the meaning

Studies have shown that, in almost all circumstances, getting people to think about the meaning of the information they are trying to remember is more effective than simple rote repetition.

Asking people to reflect in a blog posting on the meaning of their learning is effective, as is reading and commenting on the blog postings of others. But design this as an integral part of the learning process; don't tack it on as an optional extra.

Group discussions in forums, in person or on the telephone are also good ways to encourage repetition and reflection. In the past I've included regular 20-minute "drop-in" web-conferences, which any course participants can attend. These allow course tutors to cover key concepts again and help people to discuss the specific challenges they might be having.

Contextualize the learning

Case studies and examples are particularly effective in helping people to contextualize learning. Learning is cumulative and allowing people to experience it in a context that they recognize makes it easier for them to "see where it fits", linking it to their existing knowledge and making it more likely they will be able to recall it. It is ideal if you can use real case studies and examples from your organization that your learners would recognize. Failing that, fictional case studies or real examples from your wider industry can work well too.

Realistic practice activities allow the learner to apply their knowledge in a credible situation. Learning something in a particular context makes it more likely that the knowledge can be recalled in the same or a similar context. A good example is finding your way around a town you've visited once or twice. If someone were to ask you where in that town to park you would struggle to direct them accurately. If you were sitting in the car with them driving around the town the familiar sights would help you to find the car park.

Make them think about it

The more we help people consider some new fact or concept in as many different ways as possible, the more likely they are to remember it. Essentially, the more elaborate the encoding we do on a piece of information the better it sticks, because the more links we can make between it and other, existing knowledge.

This can be achieved by providing multiple examples of something that you want people to remember, or perhaps describing it from different perspectives. For example, you might show how a policy is applied in a number of different situations. Or you might show a business process from the point of view of the learner and also the customer.

An approach that researchers have found to be effective is having people read something with particular questions in mind. For example, asking people to read a case study on a change programme and identify the top three things that made it a success. These questions might be the prompts for them to write a shared blog posting.

Use mnemonics

Mnemonics (memory aids) can be highly effective. Memory champions typically use the Method of Loci[5] or a variation to achieve incredible memory feats. This method involves thinking of images that link the information you are trying to learn to familiar locations. In order to remember, you mentally revisit those locations in sequence. This method allowed Dominic O'Brien, the eight-time winner of the

World Memory Championships, to correctly recall in sequence 2800 of 2808 playing cards in a restaurant in London. Show-off!

Mnemonics you are probably familiar with include the colours of the rainbow – Richard Of York Gave Battle In Vain – red-orange-yellow-green-blue-indigo-violet. The notes on the lines of the treble clef have always stayed with me – Every Good Boy Deserves Football – EGBDF, though I can't remember what a treble clef is. Whilst undeniably powerful, unfortunately these have limited value to us. Seldom do we need people to remember a long list of words. More often it is concepts, skills and processes we want them to recall.

Test them

Some people dislike tests. However studies by both Endel Tulving[6] and Jeff Karpicke and Henry Roediger[7] have shown that repeated self-testing during the learning period is particularly effective in aiding retention. Tulving compared the different learning strategies of:

1. Study, test, study, test;
2. Study, study, study, test; and
3. Study, test, test, test.

He found the third approach to be substantially more effective than the other two. This so-called "retrieval practice" also showed enhanced results in Karpicke and Roediger's study.

Interestingly, asked to predict which approach would help them the most, students didn't feel that the study, test, test, test method would give them any advantage. Whilst this is a potentially highly effective method you do run the risk of turning off your learners with repeated rigorous testing. Making the tests engaging is one approach that can work provided you get to know your audience.

My company had won a large sales training project with a multinational flooring company. As part of the training programme they wanted to repeatedly test their global sales team and measure the product knowledge retained. We knew the sales team would not like the idea of being assessed and their scores recorded, so we designed in some game-like elements.

In each assessment, participants lay a virtual floor against the clock in different 3D locations by answering questions drawn from a randomized question bank. The questions are weighted with harder questions getting you a better score. Our original intention was to build the assessment with both global and country-level leader boards so that the highly competitive sales people and sales teams could compete against one another. Unfortunately, due to legislation in certain countries on publicly showing people's scores this was not possible. So we built it without the leader board but found that sales people enjoyed the element of competition to such an extent that they were telephoning their colleagues and challenging them to beat their scores.

Get emotional

As humans we pay attention to things that connect to us emotionally. When the brain experiences an emotionally charged event it releases dopamine, which greatly aids memory. This makes sense in an evolutionary context as an event that is emotionally charged could affect our personal safety (remember the Three Fs). This is why it seems totally crazy to me that so often anything emotive is carefully removed from training material "in case it offends someone".

I remember being commissioned to design elearning material on Know Your Customer Policy compliance for a large bank. Essentially, these are the checks that bank employees must complete on a new customer to ensure they aren't laundering money. Sat round in that first design meeting the customer knew we had a tough challenge ahead. Label anything "Compliance Training" and it immediately becomes 50% less interesting. Add the word "Policy" to the title and you can chip off a further 20%.

I suggested that we open with a true story from the news, about a young girl of say 12 or 13, trafficked into the UK from a developing country and forced into prostitution. She is made to take drugs, to which she becomes addicted while her captors make money from their exploitation of her. They launder the proceeds of their crimes through a local bank which hadn't carried out its Know Your Customer checks fully.

There was an uncomfortable silence.

Sat around in that high boardroom with sweeping views across London, perhaps it just seemed too gritty and real. I argued the point that this is precisely what Know Your Customer processes are there to do – to protect that girl and make such crimes harder to perpetrate, but the worry was that we "might offend someone". If we offended or shocked them, then maybe they might just remember what we're trying to teach them. We didn't get to use my idea. I was put back in my box.

Make it practical

We know that recall is enhanced when undertaken in the same, or similar, environment in which that information or experience was initially encoded.

That recall can be enhanced in this way makes a strong case for scenario-based learning. Giving people the theory with no chance for application simply doesn't work. Instead place the learning in as realistic a situation as possible.

So if you want people to improve their customer service skills; design challenging scenarios where they must help a customer with a specific aim. If in the real world there are inconsistencies, misunderstandings and time pressures, then design these into the learning experience. Provide feedback in the context of the scenario, so if they give the wrong advice to the customer they are not presented with a big red cross and a message telling them to "try again". Instead; perhaps they don't make the sale, they sell the customer the wrong product or they irritate them with their lack of knowledge.

I should add that, to be effective, scenarios do not need 3D environments, game-like user experiences or even graphics. Like the earliest computer-based role-playing games, scenarios can be text-based and built very simply.

You could also design practice activities to be used at intervals after the initial intervention. These can start simple and increase in complexity. If the objective is to minimize errors or increase the speed at which a task can be completed, consider having a leader board and offer some sort of recognition or small prize to the highest scorer each month.

Make it relevant

If learners don't see what you're trying to teach them as relevant to them then they won't put much effort into remembering it – and why should they! If it is relevant and they don't know it, take time to impress the importance of the material upon them, and not just the importance to the organization – the importance *to them as individuals*. Break the material up into small chunks and let the learner choose which they should do. Don't force them through a load of irrelevant content, because you'll do nothing but annoy them.

If the material is compliance-based and you need to know they have the required level of knowledge, provide short pre-assessments to each of the chunks of material. If the learner passes the test they need not go through the material. This has the added benefit of saving the learner time and so saving the organization money. If 3,000 employees only need to spend an average of 20 minutes on a subject instead of 40, that's a huge saving to the organization.

Help them put it into practice

So far we've been talking about knowledge and getting that to stick in people's heads. Knowledge is great if you're an academic or studying for the sheer love of learning, but in a work context it is performance that matters – a person's ability to do something better or do something new. Knowledge is very much secondary to that. Do you think your Board of Directors care a hoot about what employees know? It's what they can do that they are interested in.

We typically put only a small amount of what we learn in any training intervention into action. Why? Because we're busy getting on with our jobs and, despite our best intentions, we often default back to "business as usual". This is a bit of a soapbox for me; however I do think that it's utterly crazy that any training is designed and delivered without some kind of implementation plan or follow-up support. If you don't put any of it into practice then all that time, effort and money are completely wasted.

Implementation plans can be as simple as a Word document with each of the real-world skills someone might want to develop and simple steps to implement them. You might also include follow-up coaching, online "surgery" web-conferences, group assignments or goal-based learning systems.

Hints and tips

- **Educate your stakeholders:** Most people outside learning and development don't know about this stuff – and why would they? To us, knowledge of how the brain works and how memories are formed should affect every aspect of the ways we try to teach others. It would be time well spent to start to educate your stakeholders in a little of how the brain works. This shouldn't be onerous, for you or them; however, giving them a little knowledge will enable them to follow your thinking in the designs and approaches you suggest to learning design projects.

- **Measure the effectiveness:** There is no magic formula to learning design. So it is important to try different approaches and evaluate the success (or otherwise) of your work. This is a gutsy thing to do – what if this programme you've designed makes not one iota of difference to your audience's performance? In the unlikely event of this occurring, you would certainly learn from your mistakes and never repeat them.

Take courage from the fact that no project is ever a total disaster. Equally no project is ever a complete success. Even those that win awards have many things that could be improved upon. The key is to evaluate and learn from every project. This need not be expensive or difficult to do – a simple survey tool like Google Forms or Survey Monkey will do most of what you need. The only hurdle is having the courage to do it!

- **Introduce competition:** Every life-form on the planet competes against one another and with other species. We are hard-wired to do this. As humans we no longer *need* to compete to survive, but still we *choose* to compete in every sphere of our lives – sport, business, politics, academia, property, cars – you name it, there is competition. Make the most of this and let people compete in their learning. Competition introduces opportunities for repetition, testing and retrieval practice. It's also, for most people, kinda fun. Attention is a hard thing to capture and an element of competition – whether against yourself, others or the computer – can really help.

- **Make it real:** Design your learning experience to be as close to the reality in which the person needs to recall the learning as possible. It makes it more likely they will remember the information and will give them important practice in applying it. This means adopting a scenario-based approach, which at a basic level can be simple branching questions or, at a more advanced level, full business simulations. With tools like SmartBuilder and Adobe Captivate you can script reasonably complex interactions that make your learning interventions both realistic and game-like.

The usual suspects

- **Designing one-off learning interventions:** The single biggest and most common mistake is to think that a one-off training intervention will be effective – usually it won't. As we've seen, the majority of the material covered will be forgotten very quickly. Do not purchase, design or attend any form of training where there is no follow-up, no reinforcement and no help to put learning into practice.

- **Putting too much in:** People have limited attention spans and working memory capacity. Don't over-burden them with lots of unnecessary material. Cut your content to the bone then cut it some more. Less is best! Let your people drink from a water cooler (preferably fizzy and interestingly flavoured), rather than a fire hose.

- **Focusing on the wrong stuff:** If you don't identify and prioritize what you want people to learn you'll spend time trying to teach things that people don't need to know. Worse than that, your audience will squander valuable cognitive effort learning useless facts and figures. Use Action Mapping or a similar approach to identify the knowledge that underpins the skills that will improve performance and help achieve organizational goals.

- **Doing what is quick and easy:** It is tempting to follow the path of least resistance and produce learning materials based upon what you have the tools and skills to build, not what will actually be effective. You might think that having spent $1,000+ on an elearning authoring tool you should be able to use it to create everything. Beware – if the only tool you have is a hammer then everything looks like a nail. Take the time to design a solution; don't just churn out another elearning course.

The good news is that the extra technology that you might need doesn't have to cost much and quite a lot of it is free.

For example:

- You can build branching scenarios in Microsoft PowerPoint.
- Free or very cheap quiz, assessment and survey tools can be found online.
- Plenty of free blogging platforms exist that can be installed within your firewalls.
- You can pay very little for a web-conferencing facility.

It's a wrap

I hope this chapter has left you a little wiser on how memory works and what you can do to make the most of it in your learning designs. I recommend reading a few of the books listed as references to this chapter and keeping an eye out for similar publications. Unless you work in those disciplines, neuroscience and psychology studies can be tough to understand. Fortunately people publish books on these subjects that make sense of the research for the rest of us.

In some cases knowledge can strip away the mystique around a subject, but not here. The more I learn about the brain and memory the more magical it seems. Even the most seemingly simple of cognitive functions are unimaginably complex and we've barely scratched the surface with our understanding. Every one of us carries an entire universe in our heads, a universe built around and designed to serve us.

Notes

1. John Medina, *Brain Rules: 12 Principles for Surviving and Thriving at Work, Home and School* (Pear Press, 2009).
2. R.A. Nash, K.A. Wade, D.S. Lindsay, "Digitally Manipulating Memory: Effects of doctored videos and imagination in distorting beliefs and memories" in (2009) 37 *Memory & Cognition* 414–24.
3. "Action Mapping" design process by Cathy Moore. Cathy's blog: http://blog.cathy-moore .com/2008/05/be-an-elearning-action-hero/.
4. Jeffrey D. Karpicke and Henry L. Roediger III, "Expanding retrieval practice promotes short-term retention, but equally spaced retrieval enhances long-term retention" (2007) 33(4) *Journal of Experimental Psychology: Learning, Memory and Cognition* 704–19.
5. "Method of Loci" mnemonic device Wikipedia page: http://en.wikipedia.org/wiki/Method_of_loci.
6. E. Tulving, "The effects of presentation and recall of material in free recall learning" (1967) 6 *Journal of Verbal Learning and Verbal Behavior* 175–84.
7. Jeffrey D. Karpicke and Henry L. Roediger III, "Repeated retrieval during learning is the key to long-term retention" (2007) 57 *Journal of Memory and Language* 151–62.

6. Blended Learning

— · Julie Wedgwood · —

Julie Wedgwood specializes in turning the theories and strategies developed by L&D Leaders into practical real-world solutions that harness learning technology to help organizations to work and learn smarter. Julie views technology as a workplace learning enabler and believes that organizations can improve employee effectiveness, accelerate skills, transfer efficiency and improve productivity within the workforce by using a rich mix of formal, informal and collaborative approaches.

Julie has over 25 years' experience of teaching and training across a wide range of industry sectors in the UK, EMEA and the USA. She is recognized as one of the leading learning architects for blended learning.

Julie is a fellow of the Learning and Performance Institute and member of the LPI Advisory Board.

Blog: www.juliewedgwood.com
Email: Julie@juliewedgwood.com
LinkedIn: http://uk.linkedin.com/in/juliewedgwood
Twitter: @juliewedgwood
Website: http://www.scoop.it/u/julie-wedgwood
        http://www.shelfari.com/juliewedgwood

T he best learning design for a given situation is one that is efficient, effective and culturally correct for an organization. Using a combination of learning strategies and delivery media is often the best way to achieve this balance. This chapter will provide guidance on how to design an effective blend.

What's the big idea?

The term Blended Learning has been around for a long time, and many have tried to define it. In 2004 Josh Bersin[1] defined it as:

> "The combination of different training 'media' (technologies, activities and types of events) to create an optimum training program for a specific audience. The term 'blended' means the traditional instructor-led training is being supplemented with other electronic formats."

Wikipedia[2] defines it as:

> "A mixing of different learning environments. It combines traditional face-to-face classroom methods with more modern computer-mediated activities. According to its proponents, the strategy creates a more integrated approach for both instructors and learners. Formerly, technology-based materials played a supporting role to face-to-face instruction. Through a blended learning approach, technology will be more important."

Since the turn of the century the definition of blended learning has been in a state of flux and its value and continued relevance to learning design has been challenged.

In 2011, Bob Mosher and Conrad Gottfredson[3] proposed that the term blended learning was misleading and suggested that a combination of different methods and media being used in the formal delivery of learning would be better defined as *"blended training"* because real learning happens after the formal delivery has taken place, that is, when learners return to the workplace and attempt to apply the skills they have been studying and practicing.

In fact in 2008, Clive Shepherd[4] had already identified that existing definitions of blended learning did not recognize the learning that goes on after formal tuition has been provided and that the definition of blended learning should be redefined to cover the full learning journey:

> "Blended learning can integrate informal learning methods; it can also act as a bridge to true informal learning; well beyond the scope of the formalised training course, in that area of our lives where real work gets done."

Shepherd now calls this inclusion of informal learning "Blended Learning 2.0" and Gottfredson and Mosher call it "the New Blend". Unfortunately, the term "blended learning" has been used by some learning providers to indicate only that a programme or course uses elements of learning technology in its delivery, and so the term blended learning persists in being problematic as this misuse of the term has caused confusion and has somewhat diluted its value.

However, the core of what the learning industry understands the term blended learning to represent remains constant.

Blended learning is generally understood to refer to a complementary mix of teaching methods delivered using an appropriate selection of related resources, often technology-based resources.

This combination is likely to create an engaging learning experience that takes account of the subject, its context and any specific learner requirements. Blended learning is said to often be more cost-effective and more time efficient than traditional classroom training.

In a nutshell, blended learning is the antithesis of the traditional chalk and talk delivery that so doggedly persisted in education and corporate learning in the latter half of the last century.

Give me the details

There is consensus regarding the fact that "blending" should not be restricted to just the formal elements of the learning journey and with the array of learning technology now available it makes sense to extend the concept to address all aspects of how learning is provided.

Blended learning design today can offer learners:

- The ability to learn and interact with other learners irrespective of geographical location.
- Choice over when to engage with learning content.
- The ability to review content multiple times.
- The ability to explore the content in different ways.
- The opportunity to experiment and practice applying the content.
- The opportunity to engage and collaborate in discussions about the application of the content.
- The opportunity to reflect on and where appropriate share their experience of learning.
- The ability to influence and contribute to the organization's knowledge, understanding and application of the subject.

This evolving form of blended learning recognizes that learning is neither a spectator sport nor something that has to be fully controlled by L&D practitioners.

Blended learning is not about providing a linear route to capability. It is about providing multiple routes, fostering the beginning of learner control over their own learning journey and uses multiple communication technologies deployed not exclusively within L&D environments but embedded in the workflow.

This revised form of blended learning actively supports the models of Jane Hart,[5] Charles Jennings[6] and others in the move towards learning that happens predominately in the workflow and which is informal, learner led and constant. Blended learning can, and is being used by organizations to nurture evolutionary changes in organizational learning culture.

So how do I do it?

A trusted approach to designing blended learning was established in 2005 by Clive Shepherd in his book *The Blended
Learning Cookbook*. Shepherd's three-step approach has been
used as the basis for the following outline:

1. Analyse the learning requirement

The first stage of developing any learning intervention has to be research:

- What are the required outcomes?
- Who requires these outcomes? (all stakeholders)
- Why are the outcomes important? What value will be derived?
- When do the target audience need to have the capability?
- What do the target audience already know?
- Where will the target audience apply the outcomes?
- How will stakeholders identify that the outcomes have been achieved?

There are obviously many more questions that need to be asked in the analysis
phase, but it is vital to conduct this type of research to understand the drivers
for the learning, the target audience and their situation, workplace environment, existing and related knowledge and/or skills and how capability will be
measured.

Notice that the term "Training Needs Analysis" has NOT been used here. Training
Needs Analysis by its very name assumes that "training" is the answer. In helping an
organization and its people to develop, formal training should be one of the possible
delivery methods available, not the *only* method.

Notice too, that the list of questions is clearly focused on the required outcomes
and how any acquired skills/knowledge and performance will be measured.
Effective learning design should always keep the ultimate goal for any learning
uppermost and ensure that data can be collected to determine if the learners are
gaining the required capability. Being able to clearly demonstrate to the stakeholders that the investment in learning has delivered the required outcomes is
essential.

Another factor that will need to be taken into account is the budget available for the development of the learning (if any!); existing resources that can be harnessed or repurposed; any equipment or facilities that are vital to the application of the learning and which will therefore be needed for the learners to experiment and practice with and access to subject-matter experts to support the development of the content within the context of the organization.

2. Design your learning strategy

At this stage it can be helpful to decide what methods will be used at what stages within the learning journey. One way of doing this is to consider the learner experience. The model below is one that I've used successfully for many years and which I have subsequently shared with many of my customers.

GEARR (Gather, Expand, Apply, Reflect and Review) Methodology[7] was originally used by Microsoft to deliver their blended MODL programme. Charles Jennings identified the power of this methodology in 2007 and used it at Reuters.[8] GEARR provides a simple approach to separating out the content to be learned into the different stages of the learning journey. However the original GEARR Model has been adjusted below to add in an additional stage of "exercise/practice".

Whilst the original GEARR framework is said to cover the entire journey, from experience of using it, it helps to clearly segment out the different methods that are used to practise a skill or capability *before* the learner is confident enough to attempt to apply the skill in the workplace (with or without supervision). This addition updates the model to GEEARR.

Using this adjusted GEEARR Model challenges you to consider *how* the information and skills should be provided based on *what* stage in the learning journey the learner is at and the multiple ways that learners might want to *engage* with the learning. The key is to realize that the content can be provided in different ways to work in different learning situations and stages on the learning journey, reaching beyond any formal delivery and into the workplace, the informal space.

GATHER Methods – These methods facilitate the giving of background and core information to the learner. The Gather methods are often used at the start of a learning programme to provide an overview of the information that the learner needs to know about the expected learning outcomes and the benefits that stake-holders want to realize. The Gather methods may also be used to provide the learner with essential information that they must remember in order to achieve the learning outcomes. Context is the key to selecting the correct methods for the learning programme subject. For example for compliance subjects, participation with the associated Gather media may be mandatory and therefore the method selected might be formal. However, for other subjects, the learner may be offered the opportunity to gain this information informally based on their own existing knowledge and understanding and/or on their own motiva-tion or direction from a line manager.

EXPAND Methods – The Expand stage of the learning journey adds additional information to that already provided during the Gather stage. This may not be essential content, and may allow for the fact that some learners may use the skills acquired in different ways or in different situations. Information that is not essential for competency but which may augment the employees' understanding and knowl-edge of the required skill/information can be provided here for the learner to engage with if motivated to do so. Expanded content may also provide additional context and lift the content out of a set silo. For example, why train customer service only in terms of serving customers? If customer service is core to the business performance, staff could also consider their colleagues as their "customers" and could adopt an "everyone is my customer approach". For diversity and inclusivity, providing learn-ing on how to handle diversity and inclusivity issues with colleagues could also be extended to dealing with the public. Fire safety training drills could extend into diversity and inclusiveness – for example using assistive equipment to help col-leagues with mobility needs and could cross over with health and safety in terms of first aid, lifting, hazards and so forth. This content might be provided informally, allowing the learner to select to expand their understanding based on their own motivation or to meet a specific local need.

EXERCISE/PRACTISE Methods – As previously stated, in many situations it can be useful for learners to carry out practice exercises or simulations before actually applying the knowledge/skills in the live workplace and the methods used at this stage in the learning journey can differ from those used at the point of live application. Depending on the context of the subject, the methods used may be mandatory or offer the learner the opportunity to exercise/practice based on their particular knowledge/skills set, personal motivation or line management guidance.

APPLY Methods – Mosher refers to the Apply stage as the "moment of need", that is the exact moment that the knowledge or skill is being used. Apply methods depend on the content being used in context. When applying the learning, for example the completion of a task, successful use of soft skills, procedures, policies and so on, the learner may want or need to refer to content resources (media) that have already been provided during the Gather, Expand, Exercise/Practice stages of the learning journey and where possible this should be available for reference if required. It should not be necessary to provide additional new resources at this stage as the resources used in the previous stages should have provided everything needed to support the learner in the Apply stage. For example, a job aid that helps a person apply a new skill would be provided in the Exercise/Practice stage.

REFLECT Methods – Reflection methods can be formal or informal, and it is here that the power of more informal methods can be harnessed to the benefit of the employee, manager and organization. Shared reflections on the application of the learning may be part of professional development or optional depending on the learner, context and culture of the organization.

REVIEW Methods – For learning to take place Kolb[9] and others indicate that there is a need for reflection and review. Review methods should encourage the participation of line managers. In fact for any learning initiative these days, line managers are the key. If a learning intervention is provided without managerial support, all the effort can be wasted if staff are not given line manager support in the workplace. The methods used should review the impact of the learning on performance and development, measuring the effectiveness, curating newly uncovered information, and acknowledging contributions made by the learners to the improved understanding of the subject by the organization. This crucial step is an active stage in encouraging a more self-directed and sharing learning culture and in realizing the success of the required stakeholder outcomes.

Table 6.1 details some of the methods that could be used at each stage of the learning journey. Use the Content column to note down the content elements that will be shared at each stage in the learning journey using the methods identified:

Table 6.1   *Methods which could be used on the learning journey*

Learning Stage	Methods	Content to be covered
Gather	Facilitated discussion, Viewing, Reading, Listening, Lecture, Presentation, Networking, Personal curation	
Expand	Reading, Viewing, Facilitated discussion, Un-facilitated discussion, Listening, Research, Q&A with SME, Visit, Coaching, Mentoring, Lecture, Presentation, Collaboration, Exploration, Networking, Personal curation	
Exercise/ Practise	Instruction, Problem solving activity, Procedures, Practical exercise, Game, Simulation, Assignment, Test, Project, Group activity, Observed performance, Networking	
Apply	Task (on job), Observed/Monitored performance, Serendipitous learning, Learning by doing	
Reflect	Writing, Recording, Facilitated discussion, Questionnaire or survey, Test/Assessment results; Coaching, Mentoring, Collaboration, Networking, Shared curation	
Review	Facilitated discussion; Q&A with SME or line manager; Coaching, Mentoring, Shared curation, Content review, Contribution acknowledgement, Lessons learned process	

3. Selecting the mix of learning resources

With the wealth of different learning technology now available, selecting the right media to support the chosen delivery methods can be tricky and the perfect selection of medium may not be possible due to technical restraints, budgets, lack of manpower and sadly also outdated attitudes towards the use of modern technology. However it is important to note that learning technology media are not the only types of learning media available!

William Horton's model[10] for selecting and dividing up learning activities into the three classifications of: **Absorb, Do** and **Connect**, can be useful in helping the selection of appropriate media to match the learning stage and selected delivery method of a blended design as it provides a simple and practical way to segregate the different types of media available according to their most effective use within the context of the subject.

In Table 6.2, the GEEARR learning stages and associated methods have been combined with the Absorb-Do-Connect classifications for media to create a grid showing different methods and media appropriate to the different stages of the learning journey:

Table 6.2 *Methods and media for different stages of the learning journey*

Blended Learning Design Model		Media		
	Method	**Absorb**	**Do**	**Connect**
Gather	Facilitated discussion, Viewing, Reading, Listening, Lecture, Presentation, Networking, Personal curation	Seminar, Conference, Virtual Classroom, Workshop, Meeting, Podcast, Video, elearning module, Email, Documents, Intranet/Internet, SMS	Curation tool	Forum, Microblogging
Expand	Reading, Viewing, Facilitated discussion, Unfacilitated discussion, Listening, Research, Q&A with SME, Visit, Coaching, Mentoring, Lecture, Presentation, Collaboration, Exploration, Networking, Personal curation	Seminar, Workshop, Classroom, Meeting, Podcast, Video, Television programme, Phone, Email, Documents, Intranet/Internet, SMS, Virtual classroom, Virtual classroom recordings, Forums, Microblogging, Instant messaging, Shared workspace, elearning module, Knowledge bank or Curated content	Curation tool	Forum, Microblogging, Shared workspace
Exercise/practise	Instruction, Problem solving activity, Procedures, Practical exercise, Game, Simulation, Assignment, Test, Project, group activity, Observed performance, Networking	Explicit and Tacit experience	Workshop, Classroom, Virtual classroom, elearning activity, Step-by-step documents, Shared workspace, elearning, Other online activity, Multi-user virtual world, Face-to-face, Paper based or digital competency activity, Knowledge bank, Curated content, Blogs	Forums, Microblogging,

(continued)

101

Table 6.2 *(Continued)*

Blended Learning Design Model

	Method	Absorb	Do	Connect
			Media	
Apply	Task (on job), Observed/monitored performance, Serendipitous learning, Learning by doing	Explicit and Tacit experience	Use of appropriate existing performance support/curated media to effect completion of the task. (Note: all the resources here should have been provided in the previous stages of the learning journey)	
Reflect	Writing, Recording, Facilitated discussion, Questionnaire or survey, Test/assessment results, Coaching, Mentoring, Collaboration, Networking, Shared curation		Meeting, Workshop, Virtual Classroom, Instant Messaging, Shared workspace, Video, Audio recording (podcast), Photographs and other media outputs	Forum, Microblogging, Blog, Contribute to knowledge bank, Curate
Review	Facilitated discussion, Q&A with SME or line manager, Coaching, Mentoring, Shared curation, Content review, Contribution acknowledgement, Lessons learned process		Meeting, Blog, Telephone, Instant messaging, Shared workspace, Paper-based or digital feedback process, Case studies, Impact statements	Forum, Microblogging, Blog, Contributions to knowledge bank acknowledged and attributed

ABSORB Media types provide the learner with the opportunity to interact with new information that they may need/wish to acquire. Absorb media types must provide an opportunity for the learner to gain information that needs to be remembered but also the opportunity to challenge pre- and mis-conceptions, current behaviours and current business practices when relevant. Gather methods are most often associated with Absorb media as this stage in the learning journey is focused on the intake of content that will eventually be applied.

DO Media types provide the learner with the opportunity to use the information/skills in context either in a test environment or as supporting media in the live environment. Do Media types often include steps that need to be followed to achieve the learning outcomes. Expand methods are often associated with the Absorb and Do media types, while Exercise/Practise Methods are always associated with Do media types.

CONNECT Media types provide the learner with the opportunity to make connections between the information/skills they are in the process of acquiring and their own abilities, skills and situation. Connect media types facilitate the reflection and review of the experiences at each stage of the learning journey and provide opportunity to add to the provided content on the subject to progress the knowledge/skills of the subject by individuals and the organization. The key point about Connect media is the recognition that learning is not a solo activity. The impact of others on the learning experience, achievements and application when shared either within the learning group or more widely is core to changing attitudes towards the adoption of a more informal and self-directed learning culture.

Hints and tips

It is highly likely that if you are delivering formal classroom learning you will be blending different teaching methods and media together as part of your delivery. Reviewing an existing  learning design is a great way to start identifying where changes can be made to create a richer and more engaging learning experience using learning technologies.

Take a detailed look at any lesson plans, facilitator guides or other documents that provide the structure of a course or programme that you deliver and use the Blended Learning Design Model to determine the current blend in use. By using the model to analyse your existing delivery strategy for a course you may be able to:

- Identify additional method/media combinations that you could introduce to enrich your provision.
- Review your resources to ensure that they are appropriate for all stages of the learning journey.
- Adjust your method/media mix to reduce the duration or cost of the learning.
- Identify gaps in the media available to support particular stages of the learning journey.

You might consider that you don't have access to the kinds of learning technology and other resources that you might want to include in a blended design and you may not have the budget to be able to afford what you want.

The Blended Learning Design Model has been used in many organizations to review all of the current methods and media in use in the provision of learning and to consider where media can be reused, repurposed or expanded to make better use of it. Sometimes the media available within an organization for learning use may not be obvious because it is not controlled by the L&D function. Use of this model as a review tool has helped organizations to see value in resources that are not being harnessed for learning but that could be, for example telephony systems, mobile phones, intranet and internet pages, document management systems, internal communications media, among others.

Some L&D divisions that have used the model to develop learning programmes also now use the model to record the complete set of methods/media they have at their disposal at any one time, as it provides a simple summary of the possible method and media combinations available and it is easy to update and keep as a reference document for use when selecting appropriate method/media mixes for a blend.

The usual suspects

One of the problems that I experience when I introduce lots of different types of learning technology to trainers is that they are tempted to try and blend too many of the tools into their learning designs because they find them exciting and novel. This is quite understandable if previously media has been limited to traditional tools such as whiteboards, flipcharts, slide presentations and the occasional video.

I use the Blended Learning Design Model to help those who are a bit over enthusiastic to justify their selected media. Quite often, reviewing the method/media mixes within the context of the model highlights where their plans are a little too ambitious and run the risk of confusing or overloading the learner with too many choices. Blended learning is not about how many cool technology tools you can use or how clever the tools are, it is about selecting appropriate media for the subject, audience and context. Very often, less is more.

The other mistake that is often made is for a course to be created using lots of different media without considering how to bring them all together to offer one place for the learner to access the content learning resources. These days, I very rarely use a learning management system. Instead I use social media-based community spaces as I find they can be much more successful as a "hub" or central location for learners to access the resources that I blend together. As Jane Hart has said about my approach:

> "Using a social platform to host your programmes means you are able to offer a new approach to online learning where the core functionality is about sharing and interaction, communication and collaboration rather than purely focussing on the traditional content and curriculum tracking and progress."
>
> **Jane Hart, Centre for Learning & Performance Technologies**

A blended learning design is just that: a design. The design, however simple or sophisticated, needs to be tested, adjusted and tested again to make sure that the method/media mixes work. The technology selected needs to deliver the right results, and any technology that the learner will use for independent learning needs to be as intuitive as possible, because at the end of the day, it's the content that people will learn from that is most important, and the blend should support and augment the content, not get in the way.

It's a wrap

The term blended learning will probably remain problematic and difficult to define but the important thing is not to get hung up on semantics. A well-executed blend of learning methods and media that are appropriate to the stages of the complete learning journey, sensitive to the learner's situation, correctly address stakeholder requirements and reflect and/or replicate the context of the content, skill or capability being learnt to deliver the outcomes required, is the ultimate goal.

The issue is to design a blend that works. There is no perfect "blended" model, it depends on the organization, the subject, the context, the required outcomes and more. One thing is clear however: the era of "chalk and talk" learning delivery is over.

Aristotle's advice on giving speeches has been repeatedly offered as a good model for teaching:

"Tell them what you're going to tell them.
Tell them.
Then tell them what you told them."

We now know and recognize this advice to be flawed. Using only one method of delivery does not create a great learning experience. Listening is not necessarily learning. We learn in a multitude of ways and naturally blend these ways together often unconsciously. The perfect blend would be one that is transparent to the learner, where the right method and media mixes are available at the right time and place, making learning intuitive and part of the fabric of everyday working life.

Notes

1. J. Bersin, *The Blended Learning Book* (John Wiley & Sons Inc, Pfeiffer, 2004).
2. http://en.wikipedia.org/wiki/Blended_learning (accessed 9 May 2012).
3. C. Gottfredson and B. Mosher, *Innovative Performance Support* (McGraw-Hill, 2011).
4. C. Shepherd, *The Blended Learning Cookbook* (Saffron Interactive, 2005, 2008).
5. http://www.c4lpt.co.uk/blog/2011/12/06/5-stages-of-workplace-learning-revisited/.
6. http://duntroon.com/duntroon-charles-jennings.html.
7. GEARR Methodology – D.J. Clarke IV, C. Gottfredson and B. Mosher (2005)
8. http://www.trainingindustry.com/media/1640579/toolwirereuterscasestudy.pdf.
9. http://www.businessballs.com/kolblearningstyles.htm.
10. W. Horton, *E-learning by Design* (John Wiley and Sons Inc/Pfeiffer, 2006).

7. Informal and Social Learning

· Jane Hart ·

Jane Hart is the Founder of the Centre for Learning & Performance Technologies, a free resource site on learning trends, technologies and tools, which has now become one of the world's most visited learning sites on the Web. Jane is an independent Workplace Learning Advisor who has worked with business and education for over 25 years. She currently focuses on helping organizations understand the changing nature of workplace learning, the implications for their own business and how to support the continuous learning and performance improvement of their people. Jane is the 2013 recipient of the Colin Corder Award for Outstanding Contribution to Learning, presented by the Learning & Performance Institute.

Blog: www.C4LPT.co.uk/blog
Email: jane.hart@C4LPT.co.uk
LinkedIn: http://linkedin.com/in/C4LPT
Twitter: @C4LPT
Website: www.C4LPT.co.uk

What's the big idea?

It was the book by Jay Cross, *Informal Learning, Rediscovering the Natural Pathways that Inspire Innovation and Performance,*[1] back in 2006 that first brought to the attention of the learning world the fact that most of an individual's learning in the workplace is informal. In fact he referred to many studies[2] that showed that 80% or more of the learning that takes place in the workplace is informal. But in the intervening years the concept of "informal learning" has become very misunderstood and confused, so it is worth reviewing here first what it actually means and what it "looks like".

Give me the details

Jay Cross[3] uses the bus and the bicycle metaphor to explain the difference between the two concepts:

> "Formal learning is like riding a bus: the driver decides where the bus is going; the passengers are along for the ride. Informal learning is like riding a bike: the rider chooses the destination, the speed, and the route."

Hence formal learning involves learning through courses, classes, face-to-face workshops and other training or educational events, whereas informal learning happens when carrying out daily tasks as you do your job, for example, reading and viewing materials, observing activities, in conversations with people, finding things out as part of your daily work, as well as keeping up to date with what's happening inside and outside the organization.

Informal learning happens naturally and continuously every day – sometimes *intentionally* (in other words, you set out to find out about something), sometimes *serendipitously* (in other words, you find out about something accidentally, as a consequence of doing something else) and sometimes even *unconsciously* – you are not aware that you have learned something until at some later stage you realize you know something or how to do something.

But what is very clear, is that the way we learn informally is very different from the way we learn in training. Whereas (most) training content is structured and follows a logical progression through a body of material, informal learning in the workplace is unstructured, some even call it "messy". Here's a typical day in the life of an informal learner.

A DAY IN THE LIFE OF AN INFORMAL LEARNER

Jenny starts her working day by reading her emails. As she works across a number of time zones she needs to see if anything of importance has come into her inbox overnight. She scans through the list of emails, gets rid of the spam and generally gets a feel for what's arrived. There's usually something there of interest for her, and there are always a number of Google Alerts that keep her updated on her chosen subscribed topics. Jenny keeps her email open on her desk all day and receives desktop notifications of new mail – and in natural breaks during the day responds to non-urgent email.

She then turns to Twitter. For Jenny this is a key tool for all kinds of reasons, for example to keep up to date with what the people she follows are doing, as well as to receive breaking industry news. She takes a look at recent tweets, and in particular looks to see if anyone has sent her a message. She also reviews the tweets in the hashtag streams she follows. Once again she has notifications turned on, so that any tweets of interest that catch her eye during the day, she will take a look at. This provides a drip-feed of information about what is happening in her online world. Additionally, every week she also participates in a live Twitter chat with peers around the world – where they discuss issues of relevance to her profession, which proves to be a very rewarding hour spent.

Next up is Feedly, where she quickly skims through the lists of recent blog posts in the feeds she has subscribed to. Once again, she only reads the ones where the headlines catch her attention, and she quickly deletes the rest. She has learned that she needs to be economical with her time, and even if she deletes something of relevance, she is likely to see it again in some other form later. Anything she finds of value, she shares on Twitter and in her other networks, like Google+.

(continued)

During her daily work, whilst sitting at her desk, if she needs any help with the projects she is working on, or if she needs to find out how to carry out a software task that she gets stuck on, she searches Google for help – and will probably end up watching a short YouTube video or reading a short document that someone has shared – to quickly and easily solve her problem.

In meetings during the day, she discusses the status of her current projects, and in the lunch break as well as in the corridor she chats about what is happening in her organization. She also interacts with her remote colleagues in a Yammer network – where they keep each other updated on collaborative projects. She frequently has both ad hoc and scheduled (text and voice) conversations with colleagues and clients on Skype, and often works with them – sometimes in real time – on collaborative documents using Google Docs.

If the day has been particularly busy or she has been out of the office, or she has been disconnected from the internet for an extended period and hasn't had time to check out Twitter or Feedly, she will simply review the links that are sent to her in a daily Summify email (that provides her with the five most popular posts curated from the connections in her networks). In this way, she doesn't feel she has missed out on anything.

From time to time she writes a blog post in which she reflects on something significant she has learned or found in the course of her daily work – and shares this with her colleagues too.

By analysing how an informal learner learns, it is possible to identify a number of characteristics of informal learning that differentiate it from formal learning, see Table 7.1. The key differentiator between formal and informal learning, is, however, where the locus of control lies. So when L&D organizes and manages a learning event and/or solution, then that is formal learning; but when an individual organizes and manages their own learning (intentionally or otherwise) then that is informal learning.[4]

Informal learning is both a personal as well as a social endeavour, and in fact social media is now playing an increasingly important role in the way that many people learn informally. In particular to keep up with what's happening both inside and

Table 7.1 *Characteristics of formal and informal learning*

	Formal learning	Informal learning
Type of content	courses	variety of resources
	instructional	informational
	(usually) long	(tends to be) short
	sophisticated	unsophisticated
	one-size-fits-all	one-size-fits-one
People involved	students/trainees	colleagues and contacts
	teachers/trainers/instructors	peers and experts
	learning managers	
Push or pull	push	pull
Type of experience	structured	unstructured
	(the dots are already joined	(the individuals join the dots)
	up for the individual)	
Frequency	one-off-events	continuous
Location	(generally) out of the workflow	in the flow of work as a natural
	different type and/or place	part of working
Relationship to work	learning is a separate	learning is an integral
	activity from work	part of working
Social	often	sometimes
Serendipitous learning	rare	frequent
Organized by	L&D	individual
Managed by	L&D	individual
Measured by	tests, course completions	changes in performance

outside their organization, as well as to solve their ad hoc learning and performance problems. However we must not confuse the use of social media in learning with the concept of "social learning".

Social learning is learning with and from others. We have always learned socially from one another, and continue to do so on a constant basis in our personal and professional lives. As Marcia Conner, in *The New Social Learning*[5] points out:

> "While social media is technology used to engage three or more people and social learning is participating with others to make sense of new ideas, what's new is how powerfully they work together. Social tools leave a digital audit trail, documenting our learning journey . . . a path for others to follow."

Social learning is therefore not a new training trend; it is something that happens naturally and continuously every day, and just as most of our learning in the workplace is informal, most of our informal learning is social. Social learning frequently occurs when we connect, converse, co-create content, collaborate, share knowledge and experiences, and are part of a community or network. Table 7.2[6] offers ten things to remember about social learning.

In addition to the fact that most learning happens informally and continuously in the workplace, there are a number of other reasons why it is important to value it and to focus more on supporting it.

Table 7.2   *Ten things to remember about social learning*

1. Social learning is not what you make people do (as in training) – but something that happens naturally and spontaneously every day – at work as well as at home.
2. Social learning is the lifeblood of all businesses.
3. Social learning is a natural process – you can encourage it but you can't (en)force it. Social media can only help to support and enhance it. The presence of social media doesn't necessarily mean social learning will take place.
4. With social learning it's about thinking how to support it as it happens naturally and continuously – not how you can create, design, deliver and manage it.
5. Since we learn socially all the time the best social learning platform in the workplace is the one you already use for collaborative working – this might be a social intranet but it might also be some other social tool or network – but it's not a learning platform/management system that traps knowledge and experiences in a system separate from, and outside of the workflow.
6. Social learning is not about "plan and organize" to "command and control" – but about "encourage and support" to "connect and collaborate".
7. Supporting social learning means helping to build the framework for conversations and discussions around team and group activities.
8. You can't train people to be social or how to learn socially – you can only show people how to work and learn collaboratively. It means a mindshift from a focus on shaping (training) to modelling (coaching).
9. The most successful social learning stories are coming not from the ad hoc use of social media in elearning or classroom training – but from organizations that are supporting more effective learning in the workflow via sharing of knowledge and experiences as part of the everyday work.
10. Since most social learning in an organization takes place outside of training (the formal, structured, organized learning that takes place in classrooms or in online courses) in the flow of work, if you are not supporting it, then you are missing huge opportunities to have an impact in your organization.

Here are some sound bites from those who see that training (including elearning) is often an ineffective and inefficient process of learning for many in today's workplace:

- "Companies' spending on training and development accounts for hundreds of billion pounds globally each year. But every year, according to successive empirical studies, only 5 to 20 per cent of what is learnt finds its way back into the workplace." Robert Terry[7]
- "[Training] has very little impact on on-the-job performance." Will Thalheimer[8]
- "[Training] is inefficient and ineffective since people forget most of what they have been taught very quickly." Charles Jennings[9]
- "There's an inherent inertia in formal learning approaches. It takes time and effort to design, develop and deliver learning content. Speed-to-competence is often compromised." Charles Jennings[10]
- "Adult learners are becoming increasingly frustrated at how they are being treated as idiots in how they are expected to use online courses." Geeta Bose[11]
- "After much discussion and consideration we have come to the conclusion that eLearning has failed and that mLearning is moving towards a similar fate. Once a field of interesting new learning concepts and technology . . . [it] has become a wasteland of glorified PowerPoint presentations, TV game shows and pseudoscience." Kris Rockwell and Reuben Tozman.[12]

Additionally, many people nowadays prefer to learn socially and collaboratively rather than through organized training; in fact many don't have the time or inclination to leave the workflow to take training. A recent, and widely reported survey I ran, showed that whereas only 14% thought that company training was an essential way for them to learn, over 50% found collaborative working with their team an essential way of learning in the workplace.[13]

It is also clear that individuals are now using their own devices and online tools to by-pass both IT and L&D departments in order to address their own learning and performance problems. Back in April 2011, Forrester[14] reported:

"Today already 47% of business technology users at North American and European companies report using one or more website(s) to do parts of their jobs that are not sanctioned by their IT department. We expect this number to grow to close to 60% in 2011."

This "consumerization of IT" is a well-known phenomenon, but now we may be seeing the "consumerization of learning", as Jensen and Klein point out:

"Between one-third and two-thirds of your employees are meeting their needs by working around [Learning & Development departments]."

All this is clear evidence that organizations need to move their focus from creating and delivering formal learning activities which happen infrequently, and have little impact on the business, to supporting new, informal ways of learning.

So how do I do it?

The concepts of informal and social learning are being inter-preted by organizations in a number of different ways, depend-ing on what stage of workplace learning they are in. In 2010 I identified five stages of workplace learning (see Figure 7.1), which Jay Cross subsequently refined, to include the concepts of autonomy/control and formal/informal learning.

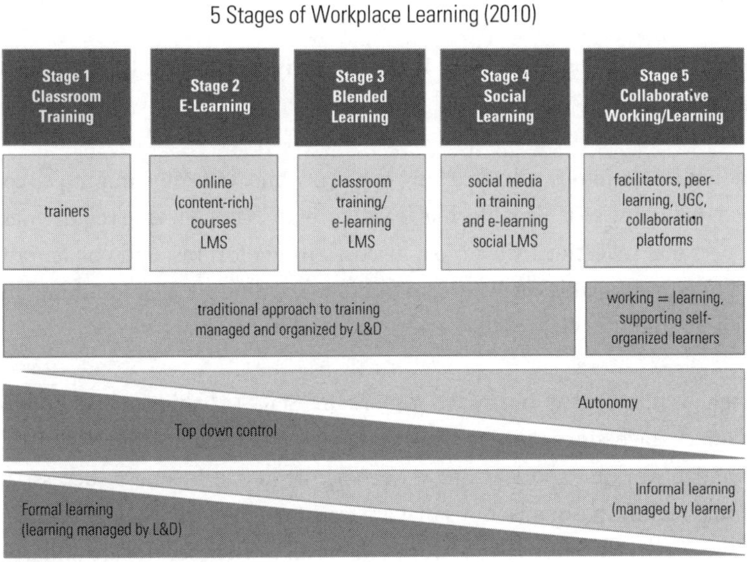

5 Stages of Workplace Learning (2010)

Stage 1 Classroom Training	Stage 2 E-Learning	Stage 3 Blended Learning	Stage 4 Social Learning	Stage 5 Collaborative Working/Learning
trainers	online (content-rich) courses LMS	classroom training/ e-learning LMS	social media in training and e-learning social LMS	facilitators, peer-learning, UGC, collaboration platforms

traditional approach to training managed and organized by L&D

working = learning, supporting self-organized learners

Autonomy

Top down control

Formal learning (learning managed by L&D)

Informal learning (managed by learner)

Figure 7.1   *Five stages of workplace learning*
© Jane Hart, 2010

In Stage 1, formal classroom training was organized and led by trainers.

In Stage 2 (around 2000) the focus moved to creating rich elearning content and managing this content in a LMS.

In Stage 3 (around 2005) there was a move to developing blended learning, initially by mixing face-to-face training with elearning, and now including a variety of resources and approaches.

In Stage 4 (around 2011) the focus moved towards "social learning". However, the interpretation of social learning in this stage is more to do with "informalizing" or "socializing" formal learning approaches, for example:

- including informal content in formal structured learning – in particular use of social media approaches – blogs, wikis, and so forth
- enhancing onsite and online courses with new social approaches, supported by social media
- sometimes embedding learning activities into the workflow – for example developing a programme which supports participants to continue to learn back in the workplace.

Although this is a good first step, it is essentially still formal learning, as Clark Quinn[15] explains:

> "Adding social into formal learning is worthwhile, but folks might get confused that doing so is also informal learning, and it's not. Having requirements for personal reflections via a blog, discussions via forums, and collaborative assignments via wikis, and more, to facilitate learning are all good things, but certainly from the view of the performer it is not informal."

Although a number of organizations are in Stage 4, this is likely to be an evolutionary stage, since others have already jumped to Stage 5, and here social and collaborative working and learning is seen as the key to business success. This is happening mainly in organizations that are transforming into "social businesses" or "collaborative organizations", that is, ones where all work processes are underpinned by social and collaborative activities.

The role of Learning and Development in Stage 5 therefore moves from organizing and managing formal training and/or blended learning to supporting self-organized informal and social learning in the workflow.[16]

Hints and tips

Supporting informal learning in the workplace involves ensuring the whole business, particularly management, recognizes the value of informal learning and that it is an integral part of working, and encouraging informal learning approaches.

In some organizations this will be a challenge since they will prefer to hold fast to long-held ideas that training is the only valid way to learn in an organization, and that it is the L&D department's role to design, deliver and manage that whole process.

So this new stage of learning and development will involve both helping individuals to become effective informal learners as well as helping teams work collaboratively.

Supporting individuals

This will involve helping individuals to develop their own personal learning strategies that suit them and their way of working.

Harold Jarche and I have identified seven key elements of devising personal learning strategies[17] that will need to be supported:

1. Take responsibility and control
     Encouraging and helping individuals to take responsibility for their own personal learning and professional development within and without the organization.
2. Get organized
     Supporting individuals as they find and use a variety of personal and organizational tools including social media tools and networks in order to organize and manage their own personal learning.

3. Seek-Sense-Share

   Helping individuals use a continuous process of seeking, sense-making and sharing, which is the key to Personal Knowledge Management (PKM) – as Harold Jarche explains:[18]
   o Seeking is finding things out and keeping up to date
   o Sense-making is personalizing and contextualizing information
   o Sharing includes exchanging resources, ideas and experience and collaborating with colleagues.

   In other words, it's not just about the social tools or forcing people to collaborate; as Harold Jarche explains: "PKM is our part of the social learning contract."[19]

4. Contribute and share

   Helping individuals become a valued contributing node in the networks to which they belong.

5. Narrate and converse

   Helping individuals to "narrate" their learning as an integral part of narrating their work, which involves regularly recording activity, achievements and reflections for others to read and learn from.

6. Get things done

   Helping individuals understand it's not about the learning per se but what they can do as a result of all their learning activities. Performance is key and that they (and their managers) need to evaluate the success of their learning in terms of their new or improved performance.

7. Reflect and review

   Supporting individuals as they continuously review their personal learning strategies in the light of a changing world, since the world is constantly changing, or as Harold Jarche puts it – "life is in perpetual beta".[20]

Supporting teams and communities

When it comes to supporting teams and communities, it might be useful to think in terms of supporting social collaboration in the workplace. Oscar Berg's Collaboration Pyramid (see Figure 7.2) shows the difference between the traditional view of collaboration and social collaboration.

Oscar Berg explains the Social Collaboration Pyramid as follows:

"What we see when we think of collaboration in the traditional sense (structured team-based collaboration) is the tip of the iceberg . . . we don't see – and thus don't recognize – all the activities which have enabled the team to form and which help them throughout their journey."[21]

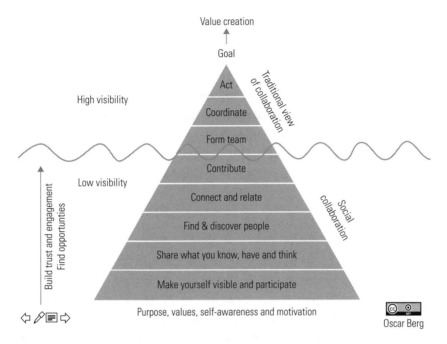

Figure 7.2   *The collaboration pyramid (Oscar Berg)*

Although Oscar Berg doesn't mention the "learning" word, he does talk about using personal networks "to access knowledge, information and skills" – and this is the same thing. So supporting social collaboration then is both about helping people work *and* learn collaboratively. This will involve:

- working with teams to help them share their knowledge and experiences within the team, to help them build their collaboration skills, and narrate their work;[22]
- supporting the set up and maintenance of Communities of Practice, by providing advice and support on how to encourage participation from all the community members, as well as how to keep it vibrant and alive;[23]
- helping to harness the collective intelligence of the organization.[24]

The usual suspects

A common mistake is to try to use learning technologies to organize informal learning. Since existing learning technologies reinforce the traditional training/course model, in that they provide course delivery or course management functionality, and are separate from the workflow, it makes sense that these collaborative learning approaches are powered by *the very same tools, systems or platforms* that are used to support collaborative working in the organization.

Key features of such social and collaboration tools or platforms include user profiling, real-time updates/messaging, threaded discussions, user groups and so forth – all of which are commonplace in today's social network systems.

In fact by supporting both formal and informal learning using an enterprise social collaboration platform, individuals, managers and others will begin to shift from the old training mindset to one that embraces a wider understanding of how learning happens informally and socially in the organization – and how it can be more fully supported.

It's a wrap

For those who are looking for a strategic underpinning for these new learning and development approaches, a number of new frameworks and models are appearing. Probably the most well-known one is the 70:20:10 Model, which is now employed by many organizations worldwide as a way of recognizing the value of informal learning within workplace learning.

The 70:20:10 Model was based on research by Michael M. Lombardo and Robert W. Eichinger for the Center for Creative Leadership. They stated that "the odds" are that learning and development in an organization will be:

- about 70% from on-the-job experiences, tasks, and problem solving
- about 20% from feedback and from working around good or bad examples of the need
- about 10% from courses.

Hence, the model recommends that 90% of learning initiatives in an organization should be informal – with only 10% being formal training.

Although some have questioned the percentages, Charles Jennings explains, it's not about the numbers; it's all about the change.[25]

"70:20:10 is not about a fixed ratio. It's a simple and extremely helpful framework for changing focus and aligning resources to support workforce development and learning where most of it already happens – in the workplace.

So, why use '70:20:10' at all? The numbers are a useful reminder that most learning occurs in the context of the workplace rather than in formal learning situations and that learning is highly context dependent. The numbers provide a framework to support learning as it happens through challenging experiences, plenty of practice, rich conversations and the opportunity to reflect on what worked well and what didn't."

However, there are other frameworks, including my own Workforce Development Services (WDS) Framework, which recommends that Learning & Development departments offer the following four key services areas – briefly described in the Figure 7.3.[26]

1. Training/Instructional Services
2. Performance Support Services
3. Social Collaboration Services
4. Performance Consulting Services.

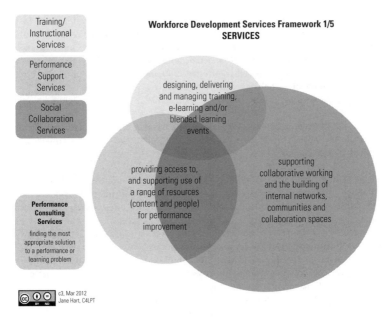

Figure 7.3 *Workforce Development Services (WDS) framework*

Whichever framework you choose, the most important thing is to recognize that the majority of workplace learning is informal. Once you do this and work with it, not against it, your people and organization will benefit.

Notes

1. Jay Cross, *Informal Learning, Rediscovering the Natural Pathways that Inspire Innovation and Performance* (Pfeiffer, 2007).
2. Jay Cross, Where does the 80% come from, http://www.informl.com/where-did-the-80-come-from/.
3. Jay Cross, http://internettime.pbworks.com/w/page/20095736/articles.
4. Jane Hart, The key to informal learning is autonomy, Learning in the Social Workplace, 27 April 2012.
5. Marcia Conner and Tony Bingham, The New Social Learning, www.newsociallearning.com.
6. Jane Hart, 10 things to remember about social learning and the use of social media for learning, Learning in the Social Workplace, 23 March 2012 http://www.c4lpt.co.uk/blog/2012/03/23/10-things-to-remember-about-social-learning-and-the-use-of-social-media-for-learning/.
7. Robert Terry, Accountability needed for workplace training, FT, 12 December 2011 http://www.ft.com/cms/s/2/ac4f71e4-1461-11e1-8367-00144feabdc0.html.
8. Will Thalheimer, Free course review template, Will at Work Learning, http://www.willatworklearning.com/2011/11/free-course-review-template.html.
9. Charles Jennings, 8 reasons why you should focus on informal and social, http://slidesha.re/gRfndb.
10. Ibid.
11. Geeta Bose, "I'm not an idiot" – a letter from an agonised adult learner, Idiot, 9 March 2011 http://geetabose.blogspot.co.uk/2011/03/im-not-idiot-letter-from-agonized-adult.html.
12. Kris Rockwell and Reuben Tozman, The rise and fall of e-learning, 7 May 2012 http://www.krisrockwell.com/?p=1480.
13. Jane Hart, Only 14% think that company training is an essential way for them to learn in the workplace, Learning in the Social Workplace http://www.c4lpt.co.uk/blog/2012/04/16/only-12-think-that-company-training-is-an-essential-way-for-them-to-learn-in-the-workplace/.
14. Reineke Reitsma, The Data Digest: How democratization of technology empowers employees, Forrester, 11 February 2013 http://blogs.forrester.com/reineke_reitsma/11-02-11-the_data_digest_how_democratization_of_technology_empowers_employees.
15. Clark Quinn, Reconciling formal and informal, Learnlets, 24 May 2012 http://blog.learnlets.com/?p=2704.
16. Jane Hart, The differences between learning in an e-business and learning in a social business, Learning in the Social Workplace, 28 August 2012 http://www.c4lpt.co.uk/blog/2012/08/28/learning-in-a-social-business/.
17. Jane Hart, Is it time for a BYOL (Bring Your Own Learning) strategy in your organization?, Learning in the Social Workplace, 20 April 2012 http://www.c4lpt.co.uk/blog/2012/04/20/is-it-time-for-a-byol-bring-your-own-learning-strategy-in-your-organization-byol/.
18. Harold Jarche, Personal Knowledge Management, 14 July 2004 http://www.jarche.com/key-posts/personal-knowledge-management/.
19. Harold Jarche, PKM: Our part of the social learning contract, 15 October 2009 http://www.jarche.com/2009/10/pkm-our-part-of-the-social-learning-contract/.
20. Harold Jarche, Life in perpetual beta, 12 March 2012 http://www.jarche.com/2012/03/net-work-skills/.
21. Oscar Berg, The collaboration pyramid (or iceberg), 14 February 2012 http://www.thecontenteconomy.com/2012/02/collaboration-pyramid.html.
22. Jane Hart, Supporting work teams, Learning in a Social Organization – a clickable resource, September 2012 http://c4lpt.co.uk/liso/liso-supporting-work-teams/.

23. Jane Hart, Supporting communities of practice, Learning in a social organization – a clickable resource, September 2012 http://c4lpt.co.uk/liso/liso-supporting-communities-of-practice/.

24. Jane Hart, Harnessing the collective intelligence, Learning in a social organization – a clickable resource, September 2012 http://c4lpt.co.uk/liso/liso-fostering-collective-intelligence/.

25. Charles Jennings, 70:20:10 0 it's not about the numbers; it's all about the change, 6 June 2012 http://charles-jennings.blogspot.co.uk/2012/06/702010-its-not-about-numbers-its-all.html.

26. Jane Hart, Workforce Development Services Framework, v3 March 2012 http://www.c4lpt.co.uk/blog/wp-content/uploads/2012/03/wdsframeworkv3.pdf.

8. Facilitating Live Online Learning

· Colin Steed ·

Colin Steed has over 35 years' experience in the learning and development field.

In 1995, he was instrumental in founding and setting up the Institute of IT Training. In 1998 his first book, *Web-Based Training*, was published by Gower, the first book on the subject to be published in Europe.

In February 2000, he was presented with the Colin Corder Award at the IT Training Awards for his achievements to the L&D profession. He was appointed Chief Executive of the Institute of IT Training in October 2000. In 2002 he was published as one of ten people in *IT Training* magazine's "IT Training Hall of Fame".

He has helped launch the Learning & Performance Institute (LPI), architected and managed the LPI's certification for live online facilitators and trainers – the Certified Online Learning Facilitator (COLF). In his spare time (!) he has published his new book, *Facilitating Live Online Learning*, and is carrying out projects to produce research, videos and further books on live online learning.

Twitter: @colinsteed

The Really Useful eLearning Instruction Manual. Edited by Rob Hubbard. © 2013 John Wiley & Sons, Ltd.

What's the big idea?

With the majority of people now able to access internet-enabled computers both at work and at home, the ability to learn online with a live trainer has arrived.

Today's learners want to learn in shorter timescales, they want learning accessible at the point of need, they want shorter sessions, and they want those sessions focused on the role they perform in the workplace.

Looking for cost savings in today's economic climate, employers are also looking seriously at live online learning too. In the Learning & Performance Institute Learning Survey 2012, 46% of the institute's members reported that they are now using live online learning and plan to increase its use over the next three years.

Contrary to popular opinion, live online training – also called virtual classroom training or synchronous training – is not new. My first experience with it was back in 1995, when I was editor of *IT Training* magazine and was invited to try out a new technology which "would see the end of the classroom". How many times have we heard that old chestnut every time something new is launched?

During the past decade or so, powered by the huge and rapid advances in technology and years of research into how people learn online, things have developed and progressed considerably. Notably, the following advances have been made, bringing reliable live online learning to everyone:

- Most people now enjoy a fast internet connection through high-speed Broadband both at work and at home, indeed even while they are travelling, by the advances in mobile technology such as smartphones and internet-enabled tablets, such as the iPad.
- Nearly everyone has computer access at work and at home, as well as owning many internet-enabled mobile wireless devices capable of receiving learning events.
- The web conferencing software has evolved into a reliable platform, benefiting from over 15 years of development and enhancement.

- We have been provided with evidence-based research on how people learn online and the best way to deliver online learning events.
- The 2008 recession necessitated every organization carrying out deep cost-cutting exercises; organizations both public and private are looking for all ways to save on non-essential costs.

And so it is, within this climate, that we have seen a dramatic rise and re-emergence of live online learning throughout the world. This time around, however, we do have a much better chance of reaping those benefits and opportunities – but only if we act on the lessons we have learnt from the past.

Give me the details

So what lessons have we learnt since the 1990s?

- Firstly, and most importantly, we now understand that the face-to-face classroom trainer cannot simply transfer their classroom delivery skills or their content into the online classroom. Although much of the trainer's skills can be utilized online, there are many new skills and techniques needed to ensure delivery of effective, learner-focused and engaging online events.
- Secondly, we have some evidence-based research on how we learn online, from educational psychologists such as Sweller, Mayer, Clark, and Medina et al. These findings prove that to enable learners to learn in the online environment we need to overhaul the traditional way trainers produce visual aids, and we must understand how not to overload our learners' working memories if we want the learning to stick.
- We need to produce shorter, learner-centred events that are focused on enabling learners to learn and practise skills that are aligned to what they need to do in their job. We need to stop dumping information into our learners – and that means a complete re-think of how we design our online events.
- Trainers need to think beyond the physical aspects of the classroom and instead create learning relationships with their learners, using the resources available to them in the online classroom. These learning relationships require the trainer to master new facilitation skills and techniques, as well as acquire mastery of different tools and resources from the ones deployed when the trainer and learners are in the same room together.

In the rest of this chapter, we will explore three major areas we need to get right if we are to provide effective, engaging and productive live online learning sessions to our learners – voice, visuals and engagement.

So how do I do it?

Use your voice effectively

In the online classroom environment, your voice is your most essential instructional tool. Firstly, and most importantly, you must ensure that you have the best possible audio quality, as this will have a tremendous impact on how learners perceive the quality of the event overall. If the sound quality is poor – choppy, signals dropping, delays, echoes, and so on – it will turn learners off immediately and will start the session with negativity.

So the importance of having the best possible quality microphone/headset that you can afford cannot be overstated. I recommend using a USB headset rather than one that connects to the computer by the line-in sockets. This provides a better quality of sound. Additionally, for good audio quality, you will need a fast internet connection. As an online facilitator, you will need to have fast upload speeds as well as fast download speeds – you can check your connection speeds at www.speedtest.net.

Apart from the quality of the audio signal, using your voice effectively and possessing good microphone techniques are important skills to acquire. A boring, slow, monotone voice will quickly create boredom and disinterest in your learners. Remember school, college or university and those long, boring one-way lectures?

Have you ever listened to an inspiring speaker – someone like Steve Jobs, Elliot Masie, Bob Mosher, Nancy Duarte or Sir Ken Robinson? All of these speakers are inspirational for a number of reasons:

- They are passionate about their subject
- They put that passion in their voice and it transmits directly to you
- They have good pace, tone and inflection in their voice
- They are "conversational" with a nice little added spice of humour mixed in

- They draw you in to the conversation by making what they are talking about relate to you and your circumstances.

One of the best ways to learn how to project your voice and make it interesting is to listen to a radio broadcaster. Spend some time listening to the radio to see how radio broadcasters have mastered the art of using their voice in an interesting and conversational way. Most radio stations have presenters that make you feel that they are talking to you across the desk – not over the airwaves.

When we speak in the online classroom we have many similarities with radio broadcasters – we are both isolated by distance from our audience and, just like them, we cannot see, hear or interact with our audience as we would in normal face-to-face conversation.

When you are online, the pace at which you speak is vitally important. Too fast and the audience will not get what you say; too slow and they'll be quickly switching on their Twitter or email accounts. When you are speaking online you need to speak more slowly than you normally would in a face-to-face conversation. But be careful it does not get too slow.

Actually, the pace you use should depend on the culture of your learners. In the US, for example, they talk much faster than we do in the UK. So, if you are training in the US, keep it pacy but not too fast! If your learners' first language is not English, then you will need to talk more slowly, and try to cut out words, clichés and colloquialisms that they would not understand – or would perhaps misinterpret or take literally.

Here are some other tips for using your voice effectively:

- **Ensure that the microphone is at the right distance from your mouth:** If you are using a headset microphone keep the microphone slightly below your mouth (in line with your chin). If you are using a stand-alone microphone, then 4–5 inches is close enough. A "pop shield" will stop those awful "pops" when you say the letter "p" and "hisses" when you say the letter "s". And remember that you don't need to shout! Your microphone amplifies the sound – so talk at a normal level, as you would in a face-to-face conversation.
- **Vary your intonations:** Nobody likes to listen to a monotonous voice that drones on and on, even when there are things to look at on the screen. As your learners

cannot see you, your voice is even more important in the online environment and it is crucial that you make it as interesting as possible.

- **Use a conversational tone:** Talk to your learners as though you were talking to them face-to-face, so use "your" and "my" and their names, and keep it informal, conversational and friendly. For example, *"How would you explain that Richard?"*, *"Laura, could you elaborate on that point for us please?"*

- **Be positive – and use some humour:** If you are sending out signals of anxiety or nervousness, then your learners will detect them. So you need to talk with authority and be positive at all times. It's good to be informal and friendly, so try to inject a little humour now and again. Balance is important though, so do not overdo the humour. While it can break the ice or lighten the mood, take care that you do not offend anyone – it's very easy to do, so stay clear of any subjects that are likely to cause offence.

- **Smile and use hand gestures:** Although this may sound odd, smile and use hand gestures as you would face-to-face, as they do alter the intonations in your voice. I sometimes get some odd looks when people pass by my office seeing me gesturing at my laptop screen!

- **Be careful about sounding too scripted:** Unlike in the face-to-face classroom, you can get away with reading scripts in certain parts of your presentation, but be careful. If your delivery sounds too scripted, you may lose your learners' attention. Change your intonations and pace, and make sure you emphasize appropriate words and phrases. Also, if your eyes are on the script and not on the screen, you may miss important feedback from your learners.

- **Be careful about leaving your microphone live:** When you are typing in Chat, your audience will hear it. So remember to "Mute" your microphone when you are not talking – but don't forget to "Unmute" it when you start talking again (it's easily done)!

- **Don't talk for too long:** Your learners' attention is difficult to capture, and even more difficult to keep. Break up your sessions with frequent interactions, but make them meaningful and in context with what you are teaching. As a general rule of thumb, if you have been speaking for more than five minutes, you've been speaking for too long.

- **Don't overload learners with instructions:** Don't overload your learners with too many instructions at once. This is especially true for smaller groups. New learners have a difficult time retaining instructions for a lot of tasks.

- **Watch the coughs and sneezes!** A tip here that I learned early in my experience as an online presenter – if you feel a cough or sneeze coming on, mute your microphone! Coughing, hiccupping or sneezing with your microphone live is a real "no-no".

Communicating in the online classroom takes on more significance and importance when you are broadcasting. Unlike in the classroom, your learners cannot see you and so your voice is their contact with you. Practise hard to get this skill right. It takes everyone many hours of practice so, whenever you can, practise speaking with a microphone. It's a good idea to record yourself whilst you are practising so that you can replay it to hear what went well and what went not so well. Today we have many gadgets that enable us to record our voice – I used my iPhone when I was practising, but there are many gadgets and even free software (like Audacity) to help you.

Although no one likes the sound of their own voice, you will soon hear improvement in your voice quality after listening to yourself a few times. As your confidence grows, it will become second nature to you.

Design effective slides

As the audience can't see you, the impact of the visual elements (your slides) is critical in attracting learners to the content and maintaining their engagement throughout the session.

I attend many conferences, seminars and courses – both in the classroom and online – and the standard of slides used by most presenters and trainers is poor. We have all seen slides that are full of bullet-pointed text, with the text crammed in making the point size so small that it is unintelligible. They are a barrier to learning, and this must change if we want our learners to learn.

Cognitive load and visuals

Before we start looking at slide design principles, it's important to understand how the brain deals with visuals in the learning context. John Sweller, from the University of New South Wales, and one of the foremost experts in cognitive science and learning, produced research on this subject *(Visualisation and Learning)*. Sweller found that working memory comprises two separate areas – one for visual information and one for auditory. When we explain a key learning point using a slide, this information is passed into the learner's working memory through their eyes (the slide content) and ears (the accompanying speech).

So there are two channels (or highways) of data – one for visual elements and one for auditory. In order to help the learner retain information, therefore, we should never mix two visual items or two auditory items. This means that it is most efficient to show a slide (visual channel) and explain the key learning point (auditory channel).

So to avoid overloading our learners' working memories, never repeat text that is on the slide. Now how many of us do that? How many courses have you seen with the bulleted text on the slide being read by the presenter? I would guess you are saying "most, if not all".

The power of images

Images are one of major tools used to engage learners, communicate content, convey instruction and promote active learning. Research from Dr John Medina, in his book *Brain Rules*, shows that people learn better from pictures *and* words than from words alone – which is not surprising considering that the majority of our sensory input is visual.

Dr Medina found that presentations that rely predominantly on text alone fail to engage and teach as effectively as appropriate visual representations. Alternatively, slides that incorporate too many decorative pictures that are unrelated to the content will hinder the learning experience.

Choosing the right visuals for the job

Dr John Medina says that vision is the sense that we take the most notice of. Therefore, we must use visuals to grab the audience's attention to help them understand and remember the content.

Dr Medina's studies have found that recognition of a topic doubles if you use a picture compared with just using text. "This is because reading text is inefficient for us. We have to read text on a slide and that takes time," he says. So the message is – you can use text for "understanding" on a slide but you must keep those words to a minimum.

Photographs also give your learners an emotional connection with the message you are trying to convey. Your slides need to tell a story and connect emotionally with your audience – and the best way to do this is to use photographs. They draw your audience, make emotional connections and prepare your learners for what you have to say.

The first thing to understand is that your learners want to listen to you – not read your slides. Otherwise, you might as well send them a document to read, right? So, the aim is to use your slide to fill your learners' minds with an image that connects to their long-term memory, and then fill in the details of what you have to say.

Visuals can be a variety of things: photographs, charts, diagrams, animations. Let's look at these and see how we can use each type of visual to enhance your message.

Photographs

Professionally taken photographs can really enhance the overall quality perception of your presentation. Choosing the correct photograph for the point you're making is of prime importance. You need to choose your photograph very carefully, so think very hard about the concept you're trying to put over and how best to represent it with an image. If the viewer can't see the context and relevance, it can hinder the learning.

As a general rule, do not use Clip Art, as it appears cheesy, amateurish and outdated. If you found your image in the clip art library that came with PowerPoint, your audience has seen it hundreds of times. Hardly going to make them sit up and listen to you, is it?

The important point, though, is that the photograph you use must be high-quality and of a sufficiently high resolution and size so that it is crystal sharp when displayed on screen. If you resize a small or low-resolution photograph, it will be blurred and have jagged edges. Please avoid them at all costs.

Whenever you use photographs that you have not taken yourself, you should pay attention to the copyright that is attached to the particular photographs you use. Read the small print carefully and abide by the rules diligently.

Here are some tips on using photographs on your slides:

- **Make the photograph as large as possible:** Large photographs make an impact, so make your photograph full size or as large as you can on your slides. A small, token picture to fill up a gap on the slide is worthless and merely decoration – in fact it is worse than that, as it can hinder the learning by filling up short-term memory with an irrelevance.

- **Use people in images with care:** Be careful with positioning people on your slides. You need to ensure that their eyes are looking into the centre of your slide – do not have them looking out of the slide, as your audience will instinctively follow the direction of the gaze of a person in the photograph.
- **Line drawings, silhouettes and symbols are often a good solution:** For maximum clarity, keep the background plain and simple.
- **Animations can be helpful in explaining processes, but they shouldn't be used for effect:** They can actually impose an increased mental load on the learner because they can impart a great deal of visual information in a transient manner.

Graphs and charts

When you want to use graphs and charts on your slides, the key is to keep it simple and make your point clearly (see Figure 8.1). So what do I mean by that? Here's an example of a slide I designed for a study on the daily consumption of coffee by the population of the world. The point being made was that, in the UK, coffee consumption is fairly minimal compared with the US and France (the two largest consumers of coffee).

Now, I could have put every country in the survey on the chart – but that was not the point I wanted to make. So I chose only the relevant countries, and produced a clean and simple chart that actually made the point I needed to get across. I could have produced a hand-out of the full results for learners to see the whole set of data but, on the slide itself, I'm sure you'll agree there was no need for that information.

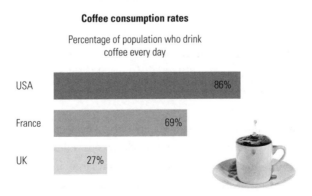

Figure 8.1 *Using graphs and charts in your slide – keep it simple*

So, when you show data, concentrate on the key learning point and eliminate the unnecessary information. Keep the colours balanced – and include a visual if you think it helps make the key learning point.

Using text and type

We have already seen that we need to eliminate as much text as possible on our slides. What text you do put on your slides should be succinct and make a key learning point. Remember, we do not want explanations (that's your job).

Fonts and typefaces

Select fonts that are reader-friendly, especially when projected on a screen. So where should you start? Well, there are hundreds of fonts available, but you should preferably choose a Sans Serif font – these are those that are "clean" without the tops and tails of Serif fonts. Arial is an example of a Sans Serif font. (Sans Serif means "without serifs").

Sans Serif fonts have become the de facto standard for text on-screen, especially in the elearning and online environment. This is partly because the interlaced display of computer screens may show flickering on the fine details of the horizontal serifs. Additionally, the low resolution of digital displays in general can make fine details like serifs disappear or appear too large.

Of course, the decision about which font to use may not be in your hands as you may be restricted by your organization's house style but, if you can choose your own font, go for the more modern-looking fonts like Verdana, Helvetica, Arial, Tahoma and Gill Sans.

Whatever font you choose, I recommend that you use the same font family for your entire presentation – you can use different font weights (like Arial Black and Arial) but for a nice, clean, professional look do not mix fonts.

And finally, ensure your text size is large enough to be seen clearly when viewed in a relatively small window in your online classroom. Files that, previously, you may have projected on a large screen may not be large enough on the smaller online classroom window. Keep the text font and size consistent throughout your session – 28 pt minimum and 32 pt or larger are ideal. Settle on one size for headings and one size for the body text.

Using colour

The use of colour is a huge topic, but these are the main points to consider when choosing a colour scheme for your presentation slides.

Colour can be used to emphasize, get attention and point the way, but it is also emotional, according to Garr Reynolds, author of the excellent *Presentation Zen* books. So using the "right" colour is an important choice when designing your presentation slides – or any screen-based learning for that matter.

Different colours are associated with feelings and, according to Reynolds, can be very culture-specific; therefore interpretation can vary depending on your audience. But there are some generally accepted associations, both negative and positive. Correct usage relies on finding out about your audience in order that you can choose appropriate colours – and of course those to avoid. Furthermore, quite a few people are colour blind, so you should take that into consideration too.

Once again, you may be obliged to use your corporate colours – but if not, why not think about the message you want to put over, and connect with your audience's emotional side?

My advice for online learning is to use only primary and secondary colours and, wherever possible, keep the background simple.

Finally on colour, as already mentioned, you should take into consideration that you may have learners who are dyslexic or colour blind. If this is a consideration for you, I suggest you look at the British Dyslexia Association website where there is a useful guide for slides and the Colour Group website for those who are colour blind.

Maximize learner engagement

Let's now focus on how to really get your learners engaged in your sessions. We'll cover some best practice tips and techniques that will enable you to grab your learners' attention right from the start – and keep it right to the end.

Rules of engagement

I'm sure you've heard the face-to-face classroom session after lunch referred to as "the graveyard shift" or, as I read the other day, the "Teflon Hour" – as nothing ever sticks. We all know it's a challenge at that time of day to keep our learners' attention and to engage them in the class.

In the online classroom, the problem of engaging learners is even more pronounced. There are so many things going on to distract us these days – emails, Twitter, Facebook, instant messaging, online games on our phones, phone calls – the list is endless, and ever growing. Learners are often shielded from these interruptions and distractions in the face-to-face classroom setting as the trainer is with them in the room. However, when the learner is seated in front of a computer, attending a live online session – either at work or at home – those distractions are simply not easy to ignore.

Although the facilitator will ask learners to switch off these distractors, we have to rely on the goodwill of each learner to do so. Whilst you would hope that everyone follows your advice, it is unlikely that everyone will. We have to accept that.

It is therefore vital that we design and facilitate the event such that the learners have to be engaged and participating in the class. The skill required by the live online facilitator to completely absorb learners into the session through frequent interactions is of paramount importance.

Let's look at some ways that we can do this:

Make it matter

One of the best ways to get learners engaged right at the start of the session is to "make it matter" for them – it's the "What's in it for me?" syndrome.

So you need to help them see the benefits of attending the session, show how it will help them in their job, show how it will save them time, and so on. If it really is important to them – in other words they can see a benefit for themselves – then they will be much more likely to be engaged.

So how you can do this for your sessions? Think about one of your courses now and jot down some "What's in it for me?" statements for the learners. Here's an example for a course on sales training. Start off your session with a Whiteboard exercise. Ask your learners to list specific problems they face during a sales call. Discuss all of the problems with the group and let them know that you will be covering how to eliminate those issues throughout the course. As you go through the course, keep referring back to those problem issues they have highlighted and cover them off as you go.

Get their attention from the start – and keep it

It's important to capture your learners' attention as soon as they log in. Use this "reception time" before the session starts to talk to them and get them chatting to the other learners too.

Using the excellent "Attention Meter" in WebEx, which tells you whether attendees have clicked on other computer applications, I have carried out a small study and have found after over 100 sessions that if you do not engage learners within 20 seconds of their logging on they will start multi-tasking. So, as soon as they log on welcome them, using Chat or the microphone, and get a conversation going: ask them questions such as "What are you most looking forward to today?", "How will this session help you in your job?", "What do you want to be able to do after the session?" Of course, you can ask anything – it does not have to be session- or work-related, although it should be topic-related.

Keep it relevant

Keep the content relevant to the learners. Use stories, scenarios and examples that are relevant to their job or their organization. For example, you could relate the current topic to a common challenge they have in the workplace. Let's say the learners come from an administration department of a hotel chain and the session is about personal security. Create the session around a scenario in the department – let's say that there has been a spate of incidents where some handbags have been stolen from the washrooms. Immediately the learners can see the "WIIFM?" factor and will start engaging – you need to keep that engagement throughout the session. So, do everything you can to keep the content relevant to them. The more relevant the material, the easier it is for learners to stay engaged.

Encourage socializing

In the face-to-face classroom, learners naturally socialize with each other before the class begins. In the online environment they may feel isolated and remain "hidden".

I have found that most people are reluctant to enter a Chat message until everyone else is doing so. It seems that no one likes to be the first! So strive to create an inclusive experience by asking them to enter something in Chat, say, *"Julia what's your job role in the organization?"* or make it non-job-specific like *"Julia, what's your favourite hobby?"* or *"Julia, how did you find logging on today?"*.

Bring your session to life

Explain things through analogies, stories and scenarios, rather than just through lectures. For example, instead of going through a four-step decision-making process, you could display a visual to match each step. This "visualizing the message" technique is a good way to engage learners and aid learning. As you build the steps, they will be intrigued as to what is coming next.

Focus on the learners

This final tip on engaging learners is the most important. Effective online facilitators always focus on the learners – not themselves. So dispense with those long introductions about you, what you have done and how wonderful you are. Remember a golden rule of training delivery: "It's not about you – it's all about the learners and their learning."

Make your sessions learner-centred

What do we mean by learner-centred sessions? Research has shown that learners must have frequent opportunities to "construct the knowledge" through active engagement.

Courses that are basically one-way instructor lectures assume that learners are able to *take meaning* (or understanding) from the information provided. This is sometimes referred to as "the sponge" approach to learning. The sponge approach – where the instructor pours out content and the learner (hopefully) absorbs it all – is doomed to failure. You are just overloading your learners' brains with information.

So we need to provide learning environments that put the learner at the centre of the experience – thereby providing greater opportunities for active building of new knowledge and skills – and ensure that the knowledge and skills are transferred from working memory to long-term memory.

Learner-centred environments are the best way to build knowledge and skills. One way you can increase the amount of time learners are engaged is to convert traditional didactic teaching sequences into inductive learning events. So what are inductive learning events?

In a traditional classroom training presentation, the instructor presents the content, provides examples, and then asks questions to promote understanding and address any misconceptions. This is sometimes called "Tell and Test" training. In this scenario the facilitator is active for two thirds of the event and the learners are active for one third if they are lucky! In reality, it's probably closer to one tenth!

In inductive sessions participants learn through examples and the percentages are reversed: the facilitator is active for one third of the event and the learners are active for two thirds. So, the facilitator provides content/examples and the learner discovers (and makes meaning of) the content and practices.

Discovery learning is a method of enquiry-based instruction and is a constructivist-based approach to learning. The method ensures that learning takes place through learners drawing on their own experiences and prior knowledge, and is a method of instruction in which learners interact with their environment by exploring.

Of course, there are some sessions that are not particularly appropriate for the inductive method, but inductive sessions are best for teaching concepts or principle-based tasks that can be illustrated with multiple examples.

Applying your questioning skills for engagement

So let's focus now on the use of questions to engage our online learners.

Start your session with a lead-in question

A good technique is to start your session with one or two topic lead-in questions. This technique is designed to stimulate interest in the topic, activate learners' prior knowledge, and help focus attention on the session outcomes. For example, at the start of your session, ask a question, using a Poll, to ascertain what experience your learners have in either attending or presenting live online sessions. Note down the responses, then choose a couple of learners and ask them to elaborate.

Another use of topic lead-in questions is to gather learners' views on their prior knowledge of the topic using a Whiteboard or Chat. Take a note of the responses for each learner and then ask them the same question at the end of the session.

For example, at the start of the session ask: "Rate from 1 (low) to 10 (high) how confident you feel about . . . (insert the subject of your session)". Then ask the same question at the end. If you have done your job effectively, those scores at the end should be nearer to the 10 by some way than they were at the start of the session.

Use open and closed questions

Experienced instructors are familiar with open and closed questions. Closed questions can be answered with a simple "yes" or "no" response whereas open questions require a fuller answer. Open questions will certainly make learners think, reason and reflect. Get them to answer in Chat, the Whiteboard and/or over the microphone.

The point to bear in mind when you design your course is that responses to open questions consume more session time than closed questions. Learners need time to consider their answers and articulate their ideas. In the amount of time it takes to pose and process responses to one open-ended question, three or four closed-ended question responses could have been discussed.

Of course, there are times when open-ended questions are more appropriate. For example, when an issue arises that is likely to have a variety of potential responses that cannot be readily pre-determined. Questions such as: "Simon, please describe an experience you have had similar to the one given?" Or "What reasons do you have for your response?" are classic types of open-ended question.

When you use open questions, it's best to use the Whiteboard, Chat, or preferably the microphone so that you can get the learners to elaborate on their answers and encourage discussion with the rest of the group.

Here are some useful tips in using questioning for engagement:

- **Use a combination of question types.** It is a good idea to use a combination of open and closed questioning: for example, start with a closed-ended question, perhaps using a Poll, and follow it up with an open-ended discussion of reasons for the choices each learner has made.

- **Open questions – use Chat and Whiteboard.** As open questions mean that you are asking learners to think and provide answers which are more than selecting a yes/no or multiple-choice option, always use Chat, Whiteboard or microphone to allow learners to express themselves.
- **Closed Questions – use Polling or Response icon.** In contrast, a Poll or Response icon (tick/cross) are best suited to closed questions, which can be framed as "yes-no" or multiple-choice options.

Be inclusive: use questions everyone can respond to

Web-conferencing software provides various response facilities: those that allow everyone to respond simultaneously, and those that are more suited to an individual response. For the most part, favour those facilities that permit everyone to respond together rather than those that only permit an individual response. For example, use the Polling, Chat and Whiteboard facilities to enable everyone to participate at the same time, rather than the Audio or Application Sharing options, which permit only one individual to respond at a time.

The occasional use of audio is recommended for responses to open-ended questions and elaboration on closed-ended responses. This will maintain social presence and keep learners alert because they know they could be called on at any time.

Hints and tips

Use the technology you have available: Most web-conferencing tools have real-time chat, polling questions, collaboration spaces and more. Get really comfortable using the tool and make the most of its facilities. With a little thought there is a great deal you can do to engage your audience. Mix it up – predictability equals boredom!

Make it a two-way conversation: Pose questions and have the group respond to them in the chat. As well as encouraging participants to think more fully on something this has the added benefit of allowing them to see and consider each other's responses.

Tailor what you deliver to your audience: Find out what you can about who will attend the event. What are their likely aims and objectives in attending the session? What might their challenges be with the material? In the same way that a good classroom instructor tailors what they deliver for their audience the good online facilitator does the same. One way of doing this is to ask for participants to submit their questions when they sign up for the session. You can then incorporate them into what you deliver.

Send reminders: 24 hours before your web-conference send email reminders to participants. It is so easy to forget about a webinar that you booked yourself onto several weeks ago. A little reminder will do a lot to increase your attendance rates.

The usual suspects

There are a few all-too-common mistakes that are made:

Too much chalk and talk: A common error is to just talk at participants over a series of slides without many, if any, opportunities for interaction. This will likely bore your audience and lead to them multitasking while you are speaking. A good way to avoid this is to ask questions and design in regular interactions throughout your session. Grab their attention in the first 20 seconds and hang on to it!

Not preparing fully: It is easy to assume that because you know your subject and you've got a pretty slide deck you don't need to prepare for your session. Think again. If you take this approach you run the very real risk of falling back into a chalk-and-talk mode of delivery. Remember it is far easier to deliver badly then to deliver well.

Having technical problems: Make sure that you test all your technology prior to the session. This means testing the microphone, computer, web-conferencing software and internet connection that you will be using. Don't assume that because it works at home it will work in the office, or vice versa. If one or two attendees have technical problems don't get bogged down in trying to fix them in the session. Instead ensure you record the session so they can access it later. If you can, have another person on hand to deal with any technical issues so you can focus on delivery.

It's a wrap

To take full advantage of the many opportunities offered by the live online learning environment, our new breed of online facilitators must learn a suite of new skills and techniques which complement their existing classroom skills. They will then be able to sense these all-important "online body language cues", and will know how to help, guide and encourage learners thereby creating engaging learning experiences.

Of course, like every training modality that has come before – classroom, CBT, elearning, correspondence courses, video, and so on – there is no guarantee that the online training session will automatically translate into learning. The key to effective online learning is held by whoever designs the session and the trainer/facilitator. In reality, these two functions are frequently carried out by the same person.

A trainer can bring real-life experience, humour and adaptability to a session, and create a comfortable engaging learning experience for the learners. In the online classroom, it can be a challenge to capture that same level of connectedness that comes naturally in the classroom. We must strive to bring that to the online classroom too.

9. Mobile Learning

· Clark Quinn ·

Clark Quinn, Ph.D. has been innovating for business, education, government, and the not-for-profit sectors for over 30 years. He integrates creativity, cognitive science, and technology to deliver engaging and effective strategies and solutions to learning, knowledge and performance needs. Dr Quinn has led the design of award-winning online content, educational computer games and web sites, as well as intelligent learning, mobile and performance support systems.

He has served as an executive in online and elearning initiatives, and has an international reputation as a speaker and scholar, having written several books and numerous articles and chapters. He works on behalf of clients through Quinnovation, and is a founding member of the Internet Time Alliance.

LinkedIn: http://www.linkedin.com/in/quinnovator
Twitter: @quinnovator
Website: www.quinnovation.com

What's the big idea?

Let's get one thing straight right at the start: mlearning is *not* about courses on a phone (or PDA – more on that in a bit). We'll elaborate, but it's too easy to take the juxtaposition of the terms mobile and learning and make an inaccurate inference.

So, then, what *is* mlearning? A simple and useful definition is the use of personal portable digital devices to make us smarter wherever and whenever we are. That unpacks quite a bit, but let's tap into the value proposition first.

Why do we care about personal portable digital devices to make us smarter? Well, to make us smarter (*hello)*! That's been the boon of digital technologies overall; they do what our brains don't do well and vice versa. Computers complement us by doing the rote and detailed things well, leaving us to do the pattern matching and meaning extraction. Mobile brings that capability everywhere. And more.

The other factor is that they're out there. Folks *have* the devices, whether cellphone, PDA, or (increasingly) smartphones and tablets. There's hardly anyone who isn't equipped with a device (or more) today. They're using them to make themselves more productive, and the opportunity is there to do more.

The state of mobile

The growth is more than phenomenal; mobile is the single fastest growing industry ever (Ahonen, 2012).[1] Subscription numbers are flattening in the developed world, not due to lack of interest, but due to market saturation. Even in the developing world 90% of the market has access, with 80% in rural areas (International Telecommunications Union, 2011).[2]

Further, even if smartphones and tablets are relatively small segments of the markets globally, in the US smartphones now outsell 'feature' phones (while so-called feature phones these days typically have cameras and web browsers, smart phones go further and add the ability to run applications – "apps" – via a mobile operating system) and such penetration is likely true of most of the developed world. Most of the audiences for mlearning are likely to be increasingly inclined for smartphone capabilities. To close the deal, most feature phones will have browsers, cameras and the ability to run custom apps anyway, so their main drawback is screen size and uniqueness.

The big opportunity, however, is the mobile platform running a mobile operating system for which applications can be developed, downloaded and run. We're talking the major mobile platforms here, including iOS (Apple), Android (Google), Windows Phone (Microsoft) and Blackberry OS (RIM). Right now, WebOS (HP) seems to have lost momentum, but that could change with the release to open source. Others with less presence exist, but the first two currently dominate the market (while Blackberry does have a big installed base, its presence is declining, and Microsoft is at an inflection point as to whether their new mobile moves will revive their flagging momentum).

Devices also range between feature phones, personal digital assistants (PDAs) or advanced media players, smartphones and tablets. Do laptops count? Most people say not, because of battery. One of the criteria for mobile is that the device is with you *all* the time. For that, the battery has to run *all* day, and laptops aren't there. And, typically, they're used for things you could be doing at a desktop, and aren't doing anything unique to where you are. If they are, they could be considered mobile, but there are some other characteristics.

Another criterion often touted for mobile devices is form factor – they have to fit in a pocket or purse or, again, they're unlikely to be with you *all* the time. Which would seem to rule out tablets as well. Let me make a distinction, and lump PDAs, feature phones and smartphones as pocketable devices, as separate from tablets. And here's where we get into a funny situation: in some ways, tablets are more like laptops, and in some ways they're more like the pocket device. Most people will take their tablet to meetings, conferences, the TV room, and some other places that they might not take a laptop. On the other hand, they usually won't deliberately take a tablet when they go to the store, a park or a restaurant, but they *will* bring their pocket device, particularly a phone.

So let's also look at how we use them. Many years ago, Palm surveyed users of their PDAs (after it was successful) to characterize use versus a laptop. What they found was that the PDA was used many times a day for very brief periods of time versus laptops which were used only a few times a day but for longer periods of time. It seems as if tablets fit somewhere in between, but I think there's an important distinction to be made.

I propose that tablets, like pocket devices, are more *intimate*. You hold them close and touch them, but they're not *immediate* like a pocket device: you whip it out, get the answer you need, and put it away (see Figure 9.1). Instead, you have longer interactions with a tablet – reading a book, watching a movie, playing a game, writing notes or making a diagram – than you do with a pocket device, but it's more for consumption or modest content creation. A laptop is really neither intimate nor immediate. And, for the sake of argument, a device that might be immediate but not intimate could be a kiosk, say for checking in to an airline, though it's not really mobile.

The implication is that a tablet is good for situations where larger quantities of data are needing to be displayed or the interactions are richer or longer, but mobility is still at least *part* of the situation. Examples include airplane cockpits, where a tablet replaces large manuals, medical situations where patient information needs to be viewed in context, and in sales calls where interaction with the customer is expected.

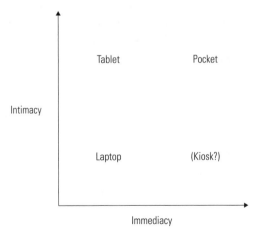

Figure 9.1 *Intimacy versus immediacy*
Source: Copyright (2013) From *Handbook of Mobile Learning* by Zane L.Berge and Lin Muilenburg. Reproduced by permission of Taylor and Francis Group, LLC, a division of Informa plc.

Overall, however, the following discussion will focus on the converged and *pocketable* device, either a phone or a PDA, that can support browsing and can run custom software (apps). These are devices that can run software, are networked into the internet and can communicate with their owners. And these are core to mobile.

Mobile principles

The core of mobile is augmenting our capability. Our brains, as mentioned above, are great pattern matchers and meaning makers. What our brains aren't good at doing is remembering information by rote, and we are limited in the computational capability inherent in our brains.

On the other hand, digital technologies have a *really* hard time dealing with meaning extraction. The field of artificial intelligence has been wrestling with this for decades, with increasing computational horsepower, and yet they have limited success. Deep Blue, IBM's chess-playing computer, could beat a world champion, but it couldn't negotiate its way to the store, as that world champion could also do. Similarly, IBM's Watson artificial intelligence system can play Jeopardy, a knowledge quiz. Can it design buildings, or even draw a picture? No.

However, digital technology can remember rote information perfectly, and compute calculations in seconds that would take people with calculators and paper hours or days to perform. Consequently, digital technology is the perfect complement to our brains. And mobile brings that capability whenever and wherever we are. And that's the magic of mobile. But there's more.

The core capabilities of connectivity, computation and user interface are the foundation to provide what I've called the 4Cs of mobile: content, compute, communicate and capture (Quinn, 2011;[3] see Figure 9.2). Three of the Cs are not unique to mobile – accessing *content*, having access to *compute* capability and reaching out to others to *communicate* – are all reasons we use our digital capability to augment our brains. They offer just the things our brains can't do well, at least at a distance.

And what mobile uniquely brings to bear is that fourth C, *capture*. Here we're capturing the local context with sensors such as imaging (camera), audio (microphone), location (GPS) and more (accelerometers, compasses, barometers, thermometers etc are already here or are coming). This is the unique capability of mobile, and

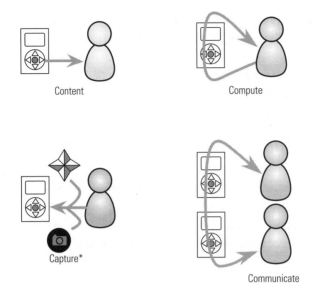

Content

Compute

Capture*

Communicate

Figure 9.2   *The 4Cs of mobile*
Source: Copyright (2013) From *Handbook of Mobile Learning* by Zane L.Berge and Lin Muilenburg. Reproduced by permission of Taylor and Francis Group, LLC, a division of Informa plc.

it has serious untapped potential. While much of what makes mobile valuable is bringing the 3Cs wherever and whenever we are, doing things *because* we're somewhere or somewhen is where the magic lies.

Beyond learning

What do we do with this? While content – and to a limited extent, compute – can be coupled to formal learning, the opportunity is bigger. I like to talk about "Big L learning", which recognizes that situations like creativity, design, problem-solving, innovation and more are all situations in which the answer isn't known and consequently they are learning experiences. With this perspective, we can think of mobile learning as meeting the much bigger picture of organizational performance: performance support and social as well as formal learning.

When you look at how people at work actually learn, the traditional emphasis is reversed: most of the learning comes with others, some comes from performance support and very little comes from formal courses. Digital technology is useful for all of these; not just formal learning, but performance support, social learning and more. Consequently, mlearning is really about all of this too. Which can be perceived as a challenge, but I want to suggest that it's an opportunity, and more.

This, then, provides the core of mobile: using the capabilities of the 4Cs to augment our capability wherever and whenever.

Give me the details

We'll focus first on the technology underpinning mobile capabilities, then start exploring the ways we use technology to support work, with a special focus on what's unique to mobile. Then we'll map the 4Cs to those work modes and explore opportunities.

Tech

There are two core issues with mobile: the hardware and the software. Each needs to be unpacked a bit to explore what we're talking about when it comes to mobile. We start with the devices themselves.

Hardware

Earlier, we characterized the devices as pocketable or tablets. Going a little deeper, we need to see what's common. At core, mobile devices have:

- portable processors with memory
- ways for individuals to interact with them (typically touchscreens, but also buttons and audio)
- connections to the network(s)
- sensors onboard of a variety of sorts such as cameras, microphones and more.

Mobile devices run software on these processors, so that we can meet those four forms of mobile activity. We can have content delivered to the screen or audio, we can interact with the device to get computations accomplished, we can use network connections to communicate and the device can use sensors to capture the local context.

Combinations of these add even more. We can capture our location and share with others socially, such as a picture of a particular problem we need to solve, or a sample performance via audio or video that we can share. We can collaboratively diagram, combining computation with communication.

Most interesting is what we can do via a GPS, directional sensors and clock/calendar. What's unique to mobile is the ability to capture our context. We can use this to our advantage in special ways, adapting the possibilities *to* the context. We can customize the information flow, whether content, apps or even connections. The work opportunities for this are where untapped opportunities exist.

Software

Which brings us to our second topic, software. The current and near future of the space is that to take advantage of these hardware-specific features of a device, specifically sensors, you need to develop custom apps. While this may not last, as HTML5 standards and/or APIs may provide cross-platform ways of accessing these capabilities, for now it's up to specific programming libraries for each platform.

Which is not to say that you have to do custom development to do mobile learning. On the contrary, short of doing sensor-based tasks, there are plenty of things you can do on mobile devices via several approaches.

The simplest way to reach the broadest variety of devices is to develop via mobile web. If you don't mind your information being accessible publicly, making a web site that is both accessible via a mobile browser and accomplishes your task is the easiest way to go. Making it available via a secure link to a private web isn't too problematic either.

The next step is to "wrap" that mobile web site in ways that turn it into a mobile app. There are software packages to do this, and you get a local app on your device that can even cache information for use when the device is not connected. This requires developers, but not the depth of knowledge required for custom app development. The additional knowledge overhead for an existing web developer isn't too severe.

The ultimate way is, of course, custom programming for a specific platform or set of platforms, for example iOS and/or Android. Here you have more control, but you also require a greater degree of technical knowledge, and familiarity with libraries specific to the platforms as well as the native language for the iOS.

So what do these capabilities make available?

Work and learning

The thing to think about is how to use these capabilities to make folks work smarter. To do that, we're going to characterize the major ways we use technology to augment performance.

Modality

When we look at how we perform in organizations, we need to factor in the transition from novice to expert, and recognize that at different stages of development, different support is needed (see Figure 9.3). The value of informal learning is small for novices, as they don't know what they need to know and why it is important. For them, formal learning is useful. However, as you transition from novice to practitioner, performing the task and understanding more of the motivations and requirements, you tend to benefit more from having access to the right information; you know what you need to know, you just want to find it. Finally, as you transition

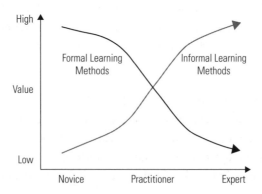

Figure 9.3   *Transition from novice to practitioner*

to expert, the value of what someone else can design is less valuable than having other experts to collaborate with.

Now if, as we said, mobile learning is not about courses on a pocketable device, just what are we going to do for formal learning, let alone informal methods? I argue for four modes, with three based upon the existing ways of using technology, and one based upon mobile's unique contextual capability (see Figure 9.4).

The first mode is for formal learning, but instead of trying to deliver the whole experience on a phone, it's about *augmenting* the learning experience. The most important flaw we see in most corporate learning is the "event" model, where we try and cram in all the learning into some fixed amount of time, be it one or several days in a classroom or in a hour-long elearning course. Instead, we should be extending the learning experience over time and space.

We can reactivate the knowledge: we can provide new versions of the concept, *recon-ceptualizing*; we can provide more examples in different contexts, *recontextualizing*,

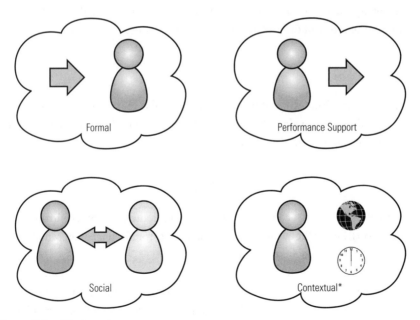

Figure 9.4   *Work modes*

and we can provide more practice (the most important thing), *reapplying* the knowledge. We can also make it more social, and more contextual.

The second thing to do is *performance support*, providing job aids via portals so that individuals can have the resources they need to perform "to hand". Here we're talking both browsable and searchable portals, and well-designed resources. It may also mean supporting self- and community-generated resources as well, and it might mean ones unique to locations.

The inclusion of *social* learning is a third way we can support performance. This can mean shared personal journals (blogs), ongoing discussions, collaborative editing, question asking, ongoing updates and more. It also includes coaching and mentoring. This is where most of learning happens, both internal to organizations and external, and through both strong and weak ties between learners and their networks.

The above, again, is not exclusive to mobile, but having that access whenever and wherever is valuable. The unique opportunity is to be *contextual*, and to do the above in ways specific to the location in time and space that the learner inhabits, and allowing the learner to share the context and situation for either performance support in the moment or feedback to improve over time.

Mapping

Taking the above framework of modes of support, and mapping it to the 4Cs gives us some guidance to consider the opportunities mobile provides (see Table 9.1). We identify various opportunities within this intersection.

Formal

For formal learning, we can augment by having content serve as introductions (or invitations) before the event, and then reactivate through concept presentations or new examples streamed out over time.

We can also produce practice items, everything from simple multiple choice, through branching scenarios, to full game simulations. Such practice, particularly if it explores particular situations, really extends the learning.

Table 9.1 *Work mode by 4Cs*

	Formal	Performance Support	Social	Contexual*
Content	Intro, Concept, Example	Job Aids, Search	Wikis	Augmented Reality
Compute	Practice	Interactive Job Aids, Troubleshooting wizards	Collaborative Sim, Editable Wizard	ARGs, Smart Wizard
Communicate	Discuss/ Collaborate	Help Line/Chat	Social Network	ARGs, Smart Directory
Capture*	Capture Performance, Augmented Reality	Share Context	Collaborative Performance	(See above)

*As noted earlier, Capture and Contextual are unique to mobile learning.

Naturally, we can provide social activities for learners, everything from having them blog, through discussion forums, to collaborative assignments. Again, this is not unique to mobile, but having mobile access can be valuable to work when and where convenient. We could also provide multi-player simulation games.

We also can do context-sensitive activities. Learners can capture performance *in situ* and share for commentary, or interview someone, or even co-create a video. You can also annotate the environment with relevant information, such as having aspects of the user's location (organizational or educational) available for inspection, maps and more.

Performance support

For performance support, we see similarly rich opportunities. We can have static job aids available, as well as supporting search of the organization resources. We can have interactive job aids or wizards available on tap as well.

For social performance support, we can have connections to experts via text or voice in a variety of ways. We can also have access to a network of peers. Contextually, we can pre-configure the information or people who might connect to be relevant to where or when we are.

Social

For social learning, we can connect learners to wikis for collaboratively created content resources, and eventually I think we'll see community-generated wizards, where the information is determined by the community itself. We could also see multi-player simulation games.

Of course, the real power here is to be able to reach out to our social network for pointing to interesting things, asking and answering questions, finding the right expertise and more.

Finally, contextually, we can be working together whenever and wherever we need to be to accomplish a task.

Contextual

Augmented reality is annotating the world with additional information, whether visual or auditory. We can make available unique bits of text, diagrams or audio to be accessed in a particular location, which is relevant to the learner for a particular learning or performance goal they have.

We can also have available Alternate Reality Games (ARGs), leveraging our mobile devices. ARGs posit a "story" that leaves traces via real and digital "clues" such as web sites or messages as if real, and allows us to interact with them. We can co-opt this learning approach by designing experiences distributed across reality which put the learner(s) in positions to make decisions similar to the ones they have in the real world, using the technologies we increasingly use to interact with others and gather information. We could also have wizards that are sensitive to the local location.

Similarly, for social, we can have directories that are sensitive to the location of the performer, or semantically related to their task (for example if a sales person is meeting with a pharmaceutical company, a member of the pharmaceutical practice would be prioritized in a list of resources).

This perspective provides the core thinking behind mobile. How do we go about it?

So how do I do it?

Designing mlearning at the tactical level is little different than designing other interventions – you need to know what you're trying to achieve, design a solution, develop it and test it. Rinse and repeat. However, there are unique facets to developing mobile solutions, and given that we're talking about a broader space of support, we need to talk about a broader approach. We also have the broader context of the mobile strategy as well. While a one-off project isn't a bad thing to get some initial experience you really should be taking a strategic approach.

Strategy

Mobile isn't like just getting new software, it's more like deciding what computers the company is going to support. As such, it's a much bigger issue than just "let's do an app". We need to treat the whole process as a platform approach. While this is a topic for a book, not just a part of a chapter, let me outline some of the unique components for mobile.

In general, for a strategy, we need a number of components (see Figure 9.5). These components include a vision of what you're trying to do, your strategy as a sequence of goals and associated tactics, your metrics for success, your partners, messaging around the strategy, schedule for delivery, budget, resources including human, and associated skilling of the latter.

These generic elements play out in particular ways for mobile. While your vision and schedule will be unique, there are some elements that have particular roles for mobile in the other components (see Table 9.2). Your goals will be aligned with and in support of the overall organizational strategy, as well as the unit goals implementing the mobile strategy. The tactics include those work modes mentioned earlier. Your resources will include capabilities around devices, mobile-specific tools and infrastructure, and designers and developers (whether in-house or not). The skilling requirement will be to not only come to grips with the differences mobile introduces (for example UI, platform) but also the rapid changes in a still-dynamic field, as well as managing in this new environment. The messaging for the mobile

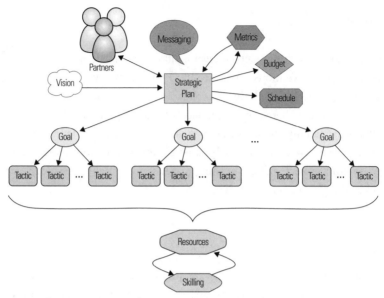

Figure 9.5   *Strategy components*

move needs to address the advantages to be gained, as well as the unique issues that will be faced. And the partners will potentially be more integrated with folks like HR, IT and even legal.

To start with, you've some information gathering to do. What devices characterize your target audience already? Are any devices already issued by the organization? What's the context of performance: are there constraints on connectivity, on mobility or on security?

You'll also want to ascertain the appetite of the organization for mobile. Can it and will it become a sizeable proportion of the performance solution set? In many ways, that may make sense, as mobile is appearing as a game changer. Recognize that most toolsets are likely to be mobile capable soon if they're not already so, so you may not need to fully prepare for sophisticated mobile development, but in many cases that may make sense.

You'll also need to be making some policy decisions: what platforms are you going to support, and how will you help people meet those requirements? Will you use

Table 9.2 *Mobile strategy*

Strategy Element	Mobile Considerations
Goals	Augmenting Org Strategy Unit Goals
Tactics	Augmenting Formal Learning
	Performance Support
	Social
	Context-sensitive
Resources	Devices
	Tools
	Infrastructure
	Designers
	Developers
Skilling	Tools
	Support
	Designers
	Developers
	Managers
Messaging	Advantages
	Issues
Partners	IT
	HR
	Vendors
	?
Metrics	Access
	Unique Contribution

"BYOD" (Bring Your Own Device) or provide a platform or a limited set? There are no "right" answers, only tradeoffs, but you'll want to make a decision that works for the long term. Providing a device, while initially expensive, makes it easier to develop for a known platform, and helps remove the barriers individuals might face in using their own devices for work purposes.

The important thing is to realize that once you support a solution for a particular need, you've opened the door to more, so you want to take a platform approach. And you need an associated platform-level strategy. It may even end up being the case that for some business units, special devices are provided, with BYOD rules for other parts of the organization, but you want to make that determination on principled grounds, not ad hoc and independent of other units.

This will interact with other activities going on in the organization, and may provide opportunities. If there's a portal, content management, knowledge management, learning management, or social media system initiative, you should see what extra overhead there is for the mobile option to be enabled. Such initiatives may provide the opportunity to add mobile capability to support workflow with marginal extra investment.

A second such strategic position goes around content development, whether it be tools or outsourcing to vendors. Are the processes mobile-capable? Everything being developed going forward should be mobile compatible. Why wouldn't you want to have the information available if an individual would find it useful?

Note that this means that the organization as a whole really ought to have a mobile strategy. The benefits are that the instigators will be seen to be taking a responsible role in strategy. The possible challenges are credibility amongst the appropriate executive level, and the ability to play a role in the decision process. Establishing good relations with IT will be a necessary component.

In short, mobile-accessible is now a criterion in all technology initiatives. If it's not mobile available, it shouldn't be an option. When companies like Google say they're going "mobile first" (Gundotra, 2010),[4] it's a wake-up call.

Once you've ascertained your platform and strategy, you can get into the tactics of developing specific solutions.

Tactics

If we're talking about looking at a full spectrum of solutions, we need to start from a bigger perspective than a course. We need to identify what the need is, and what the opportunity is. In one instance I was asked in to work with a company that had already developed a couple of mobile apps and they were looking for support in brainstorming new ideas. I initially asked whether social would be an option, and was told "no", yet during the session the ideas they kept coming up with as most valuable were social! The point being that when we move to "Big L" learning (looking at innovation, creativity, problem-solving, design), we're talking about a richer suite of interventions than just courses.

Still, most design processes share roughly the same steps. While most of the readership may be familiar with the ADDIE (analyze-design-develop-implement-evaluate) Model, the ADDIE Model *assumes* a course is the answer, so we need another framework. I've looked at design models across other fields, and found three-step, five-step, and other models. I've preferred to use one that folks from other fields understand as well (and developers and other people also play a role in this), so the framework I use talks about an iterative process of *analysis* of the situation, *specification* of a potential solution, *implementation* of the proposed intervention and *evaluation* of the outcomes (see Figure 9.6). Here we'll go through each of the steps, discussing what's unique to mobile.

Analysis

To start, you must focus on the business need. What is the area of business for people *not* in the office (and know that when you're making a site visit, at a conference, even just in a meeting but not at a desk, you're a mobile worker) that, if changed, would yield a big impact on the organization? Then you want to figure out what the nature of the intervention or change *should* be.

You'll need to have a broader repertoire than just courses, and have to determine whether this is an opportunity for a mobile solution. *When* formal learning is the

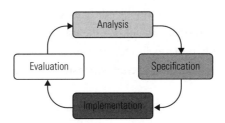

Figure 9.6 *Four steps of development*

best solution, for example when your learners are novices, mobile can come into play as a way to augment the learning by extending the experience. If it's when folks are away from a desk and need support, then mobile is definitely an opportunity.

What's different here is that you'll need to look more closely at the profile of the learners and the context in which they are performing to determine your approach. Is this an environment in which there's connectivity? Who else is involved? What resources are available in the environment? This is in addition to existing decisions about the audience and required performance.

You should also identify what the business impact you need is, quantitatively. This has several benefits. For one, you'll align your design to the business need. Two, you'll have concrete criteria for evaluating your design and knowing when you can stop iterating (the right answer for when to stop is *not* "when you run out of time and/or money").

Specification

Once you've identified a need, in terms of audience, performance context and gap, you can start determining an approach. As always, you'll want to diverge before you converge on your solution.

Here, focus on what specific mechanism from the modes listed above (formal, performance support, social or contextual) to include. Alternatives to be considered are augmenting formal learning, providing performance support or enabling social connections. You also should be thinking about whether to use content, compute capabilities, and whether you'll try to make it contextually relevant.

Mobile-specific issues in the solution include bandwidth and usability. The latter, in particular, is critical for mobile. It's not just the user interface, but the information architecture as well. When there's limited information space available, making the navigation both comprehensible and comprehensive is crucial.

Note that you should be, at this stage if not at analysis, specifying the metrics for evaluation. You'll use your business impact metrics from the analysis phase first, but you need a bit more detail. You'll want to supplement the business impact metrics with both the usability metrics you expect, and any subjective experience goals you have. The latter, in particular, are normally just subjective, but you should set your desired user experience from an engagement or satisfaction perspective as well.

Implementation

The implementation picture changes almost daily in terms of development environment. In addition to deciding whether to go for mobile web, wrapped mobile web, or custom app development, you have to end up converging on a particular tool suite. The dynamism of the field precludes recommendations here (they'll be out of date by the time this book is in print), but some overall guidance is possible.

First, postpone programming, and prefer paper (the double double Ps). Prototype is the lowest technology you can have to get the answers you need. Sticky notes, note cards and so forth are great. Many packages now exist to do wire-framing graphics on screen and onto paper that don't require programming. You should be iterating with as low a cost as possible as late as possible.

Once you lock in to a design, then get technical. Be aware that many standard toolsets are moving to support mobile devices, so see if one of your existing tools outputs to mobile. Or consider a package of generic mobile capability, such as a content delivery system. In general, you should match your investment in a delivery platform to the level of capability you need, but do so with a mind to your overall plans, not just immediate.

That said, it may be that if your mobile plan is to make it a growing part of your core capability, you may well want to use industrial-strength tools even for initially small projects to develop your capability. Your strategy will determine the viability of this approach.

Evaluation

Like any intervention, you should be evaluating the impact to determine when you've achieved your goals. You'll be making a three-way decision: it's working, we're done; it's not where we want so we either tweak the solution or our criteria; it's just not working and we should stop now. The mobile-specific parts include, again, the usability, the impact, and the user experience.

You should be iterating quickly, testing questions you don't have answers to (will it work better this way or that?) You might be exploring interface alternatives (tabs at bottom or top), and definitely should be responding to feedback from test users.

You should be looking at data from sites that evaluate mobile usage, as well as user feedback (focus groups, interviews and so forth). Observation of people in action is another recommended approach. Particularly until you get familiar with the dimensions of mobile, you'll want to immerse yourself in their world, not just at analysis time, but also again during testing.

At some point, you'll be moving from the three-way question to a two-way: no/go. Not that a project should ever be finished; you should be reviewing your interventions from time to time, and deciding when they should be shelved, as nothing's likely to be valuable *forever*.

Hints and tips

In addition to the general design process, certain guidelines are worth keeping in mind with regard to mlearning success. The hints and tips here focus on principles, pragmatics and process.

Features

Minimalism

One of the first principles I like is the "least assistance" principle. Another way to put it is "what's the least I can do for you?" This is not to be rude, but instead keeps the focus on finding the amount of help that's least intrusive and provides the one thing to get them past their barrier.

Another way to reframe the least assistance principle is to tap into John Carroll's minimalist instruction approach (Carroll, 1990),[5] which was really focused on performance support. In it, he tried to find the minimal amount of support needed to help performers succeed at their task.

It turns out that minimalism also works in two other important ways. The first is that accessibility is aided by minimalism, to the point where the W3C (the World Wide Web Consortium that governs standards) says "Web sites can more efficiently meet both goals when developers understand the significant overlap between making a Web site accessible for a mobile device and for people with disabilities" (W3C, 2008).[6] The second is that minimalism is also valuable for most web and elearning content, so the efforts to develop habits in this area pay off in other work.

80/20

Another, related, principle, is to design the 20% of the capability that meets 80% of the needs (also known as the Pareto principle). As documented in *The Zen of Palm* (PalmSource, 2003),[7] "Focus on what users do 80 percent of the time", mentioning how the Palm Datebook app took you to the current date, as that's what people typically were looking for.

A mobile app shouldn't try to accomplish all of what a desktop app can and should do. For example, complex processing of audio, graphics, video, etc. will stress the user interface of a mobile device, let alone the processor and consequently the battery life. The whole reason Apple resisted Flash was not a bunfight with Adobe, but because if Flash was running it was so processor-intensive, you wouldn't be able to get a whole day's use out of your mobile device, and thus violated user expectations and undermined the user experience.

Figure out what the core needs are, and focus on meeting those. Some of this will turn out to be a consideration of what needs to be done in the field, and what will wait 'til back at the office. Technically, it may also be what will be done locally and what should be handled via a server.

Process

Usability

A related issue is to be careful on usability. The more complex interactions required, with limited interfaces both for input and for the device communicating to the user, means more focus has to be put on design. This includes making things available, hiding what may not be needed initially and brought on demand, and helping the learners with navigation, letting them know where they are in the application and how they can get to other information or capabilities.

Similarly, the information architecture, laying out where functionalities are and how you get to them, is also important. You need to spend considerable time being detailed on this.

Ethnographic analysis

One particularly useful step is to visit and observe the performance environment. Take an ethnographic approach by investigating how your audience performs in the work context, and observe in detail, in ways that are as unintrusive as possible. Travel with the audience and see the context before, during and after use of the mobile application.

The purpose is to truly understand the task and variability, to develop solutions that will work under real conditions. This can be accompanied by videotaping, or just serious note taking, but such detailed work is necessary.

Use cases

A valuable trick at this point is to employ use cases, where you define specific users and their goals. Once you've specified the goal, you can specify the steps to achieve that goal through your design, with a focus on minimizing steps. Being concrete helps figure out what the suite of capabilities should be and how to deliver them. One guide is that learners should be no more than two clicks and 10 seconds from their goal.

Pragmatics

Low-hanging fruit

One of the things to think about is how to leverage what you already have. If you've got content already (and most organizations are quite content-rich), is it mobile accessible, or how much could be made mobile accessible?

Most existing content – documents, videos, audio files – can be viewed on mobile devices, at least if it's been converted to an appropriate format. You should be doing two things: building mobile formats into your content production processes, and considering how to systematically (and with low overhead) make your existing resources accessible.

Focus on those most likely to be used while "on the go", such as job aids for performance out in the field, and convenient access: podcasts or videos that individuals might want access to when convenient. One engineering firm recognized that groups of engineers were writing white papers that others would have liked to have seen but weren't finding the time. The L&D group had the white papers read into audio files for them to listen to while commuting, and the engineers came back and demanded more!

Doubters

There will undoubtedly be folks who are resistant to the mobile enchantment. While the evidence of the overwhelming growth is one argument, a second is much more pragmatic – their own experience.

Ask them about their mobile usage. How do *they* use mobile devices? Odds are, they snap pictures, use a calculator or a browser, take voice memos, store music, or other things, and that's just a feature phone! If it's a smartphone, they'll have a suite of apps they use.

Making it personal helps them see how useful these devices actually are. Of course, you also have to sensitize doubters to the fact that it's not about courses, but you can ask how many courses they've taken on their mobile device. (Thanks to Craig Taylor for this one.)

The usual suspects

As well as hints and tips, there are some things to be avoided. Included here are having too narrow a focus and considering a too-limited suite of solutions.

Putting elearning on a phone

The first way organizations go awry, despite the admonition at the start of the chapter *and* by pretty much all the mlearning advocates out here, is thinking that mlearning is about courses on a phone. To be fair, elearning vendors are making mobile output for their course tools, or new tools for making mobile versions of courses, which means it's easy to make the mistake, but it's still a mistake.

There *might* be a case for elearning on a tablet as it's got enough screen, and is more appropriate for longer engagements. However, you'd still want to minimize it (which isn't a bad call for most elearning anyway), and of course you want to take advantage of the touch screen.

Please, *please*, don't just convert your existing elearning courses to run on tablet, let alone a phone. If you must, and there have been (few) success stories (for example compliance training), then slash it to the bare minimum, and beyond. Your learners will thank you.

Thinking "content"

There's nothing wrong with content, *per se*, but we too often prematurely converge on that as a solution, when other solutions are possible, and may be preferable. Think through the 4Cs, at least.

First, think about a job aid instead of a course. Use the least you need to! And think of media beyond text, as well. When would audio or video be more effective?

Then, think about something interactive rather than passive. Beyond just reconceptualizing and recontextualizing, reapplication is a deeper form of reactivation. Similarly, a wizard may be more helpful than just a passive checklist or process map.

Finally, consider whether connecting to the right person might be better than trying to create a canned bit of content. The network is the way of the future, and as folks like my Internet Time Alliance colleagues (including two co-authors in this book) will tell you, as things move faster, trying to codify the knowledge will not be able to cope.

Making assumptions about devices

Don't assume you know what devices your audience is using, the answer might surprise you. Whatever you think they have: cellphones, smartphones, tablets, test your assumptions.

The variety of devices is growing by leaps and bounds. Think they're all on iOS? Android is more prevalent than iOS by quite a bit, and has been for a while. Think they're not on Blackberries? Blackberry is still prevalent in the workplace (though declining). Think they're not using smartphones yet? Smartphones have already surpassed the sales of feature phones, at least in the US.

The point is, your assumptions may be out of date. Do check. (Thanks to Ryan Tracey for this.)

Prematurely converging

It's going to be easy to decide "we need an app", or conversely "mobile web is good enough", but either assumption can be off. There are times when each makes sense, of course, but explicitly considering both, and the relative benefits and costs, should be valuable.

Mobile web is easy, as indicated above, but has limitations. If you think more broadly about what you might be able to add with an app, you could find some real opportunities.

Conversely, thinking you have to have an app may prematurely lock you in to a more expensive option than you might actually need. Apps certainly have more features, but the things that mobile web (wrapped or not) can do are increasing by leaps and bounds.

The point is not to say you won't have to choose eventually, but instead to make sure you've explicitly considered both and then made the decision consciously with appropriate diligence. Then you can choose with a clear conscience.

One-offs rather than platform

It's tempting to get a mobile app up for a variety of reasons. To get some experience, to be seen to be on top of the latest moves, and, not least, to actually be meeting a real need. And, for all those reasons, an initial app isn't a bad idea. However, at least in parallel, you should be looking at the platform.

Mobile isn't a fad, it's a trend, if not an out and out revolution. Consequently, you want to be prepared for a major shift to mobile augmentation. Mobile is not tactical, it's strategic. Yes, it aligns with the organizational strategy, but it needs to be dealt with in a coherent way.

It's a wrap

Mobile is a major shift. It's changing things socially, commercially, and organizationally. Socially, you know it's a serious conversation when your conversant places their phone on the table and turns it off. Commercially, shoppers are now sending pictures of themselves in clothing and soliciting suggestions, rather than shopping in a group. And organizationally, the social media cigarette break is being seen around organizations that block social media access through the firewall. You can't stop the signal!

It's time to get onboard the mobile train. It may have a bit of hype bubble associated, but the fact of the matter is that these devices aren't going away – the convenience is just too much. The question then becomes how to cope.

You cope by getting strategic, and getting started. The time is well and truly *now*.

Mobilize your forces!

Notes

1. T. Ahonen, TomiAhonen Almanac 2012 http://communities-dominate.blogs.com/brands/2012/02/the-state-of-the-union-blog-for-mobile-industry-all-the-stats-and-facts-for-2012.html.
2. International Telecommunications Union (2011). ICT Facts and Figures. http://www.itu.int/ITU-D/ict/facts/2011/material/ICTFactsFigures2011.pdf.
3. C. Quinn, *Designing mLearning: Tapping Into the Mobile Revolution for Organizational Performance* (San Francisco: Pfeiffer, 2011).
4. V. Gundotra, Barcelona: Mobile First, 2010. Google Mobile Blog. http://googlemobile.blogspot.com/2010/02/barcelona-mobile-first.html.
5. J.M. Carroll, *The Nurnberg Funnel: Designing Minimalist Instruction for Practical Computer Skill* (Cambridge, MA: MIT Press, 1990).
6. W3C, *Web Content Accessibility and Mobile Web: Making a Web Site Accessible Both for People with Disabilities and for Mobile Devices*, 2008 http://www.w3.org/WAI/mobile/.
7. PalmSource, *The Zen of Palm*, 2003 http://www.accessdevnet.com/docs/zenofpalm/Enlightenment.html.

10. Game-Based Learning

· Ben Betts ·

Ben Betts is a gamer, entrepreneur and learning geek. He combines his passions to create social and game-based learning projects with his company, HT2, working with organizations in the UK and USA to create learning experiences with impact beyond their means. His clients include Google, BP, Barclays, NHS, KPMG, Duke CE, Pearson Education, Cambridge University, Oxford University and many more.

Ben has studied at Exeter, Liverpool and Warwick universities, with varying degrees of success. His MBA concentrated on the process of change within large organizations. His doctoral research focused on the creation of a new model of workplace elearning based on gamification principles. Today, Ben researches, writes and speaks widely on gamification and games for learning.

Email: ben@ht2.co.uk
LinkedIn: http://uk.linkedin.com/in/benbetts
Twitter: @bbetts

What's the big idea?

*"Playing a game is a voluntary attempt to overcome
unnecessary obstacles."*

Bernard Suits

Computer games are no longer the domain of geeky teenage boys. The average age of a gamer is said to be early to mid-thirties. Nearly half are female. Increasingly, games are becoming a focal point for the development of new elearning interventions under the mantra of "game-based learning" or "serious games".

Games for learning have been shown to be effective in academic studies stretching back over the last 30 years. Simon Egenfeldt-Nielson and Traci Sitzmann compiled separate studies reviewing the evidence from more than 80 projects to conclude that students using games for learning tended to show an improvement in the attainment of learning objectives when compared to students using more standard instructional methods. This shouldn't come as a surprise; we know that being active in a learning experience is more effective than remaining passive and games demand our active attention. Advocates of game-based learning suggest that games create deeper learning experiences that more thoroughly engage participants in the attainment of learning objectives – motivated learners retain more than their uninterested counterparts.

However, just because we could use games for learning, doesn't mean we should. One of the biggest blockers is the sheer cost of creating a game. Authors like Marc Prensky[1] suggest that digital game-based learning projects tend to cost something in the order of $1m to develop. Traci Sitzmann[2] quoted figures in the multi-millions for those games she studied. This is bonkers. Game-based learning can be achieved on budgets similar to most other elearning projects, sometimes even less. You don't need to build a virtual world to rival "Call of Duty" to make a game for learning.

This chapter will take a holistic view of the current game-based learning landscape, taking you on a journey through some of the design principles that underpin games and highlighting the game genres that can be used most effectively in a learning environment.

Give me the details

Game-based learning isn't an easy beast to pin down in terms of a single, widely accepted definition of the phrase. The blame for this falls at game designers' feet who can't decide on a definition of a game either. What *is* more widely accepted is that the term "game" is useless. Because games can be so widely different, their classification as a single entity becomes somewhat irrelevant.

Jesse Schell, a game designer and educationalist of high regard, suggests that a game can be defined as "a problem solving activity, approached with a playful attitude".[3] I really like this definition, but the "playful attitude" part of Schell's definition can cause some consternation amongst game-based learning practitioners as it gives the impression of games always being fun. Others avoid the "fun" issue by ignoring it altogether, for example, Tracy Fullerton suggests that a game is a "closed, formal system that engages players in a structured conflict and resolves its uncertainty in an unequal outcome".[4]

Jane McGonigal suggests that games have four defining features:

1. "A goal, which players work to achieve.
2. The rules, which represent the constraints within which players must accomplish their goal.
3. The feedback system, which allows players to evaluate their progress towards the goal.
4. Voluntary participation; that players accept the goal, the rules and the feedback system and do so in an autonomous environment".[5]

Neither of those definitions mentions the word fun but they do perhaps allude to an attitude of playfulness – a willingness to be light-hearted with an activity. Playfulness is perhaps a defining feature of what makes game-based learning so useful; that participants are willing to try new behaviours. This gets to the heart of learning and development as a practice and is something we should aspire to in all of our interventions.

Fun, on the other hand, is not quite the same. Fun isn't something you can order people to have. And fun comes in many forms; Marc LeBlanc[6] articulates eight types of fun that can be readily identified in games. What we are interested in most might be called "hard fun"; fun that is derived from accomplishment and is manifested when you learn something new. For Raph Koster, author of the genre defining book "A theory of fun for game design", this concept of fun gets to the very core of what makes games so engaging; they give us the opportunity to apply our learning in order to win.

But perhaps my favourite definition of a game comes not from the point of view of the game designer, but from that of the game player. Bernard Suits wrote that "playing a game is a voluntary attempt to overcome unnecessary obstacles".[7] Whilst we can be a somewhat sedentary species, humans have always felt the urge to challenge themselves, to achieve a higher state of mastery. We don't always do this willingly, but interestingly enough, tougher challenges seem to engage us more readily than mundane ones.

Game-based learning can build on this definition to form one of its own: game-based learning is the use of digital games in the pursuit of purposeful learning goals. That we might need to overcome some unnecessary obstacles along the way is, literally, part of the fun.

So how do I do it?

When was the last time you played a computer game? If the answer is more than seven days ago, consider this your permission slip to go play. If you want to implement a game-based learning approach then you need to be playing computer games. Clark Aldrich, a serious games expert, advocates downloading a popular $1.99 game from an app store every couple of weeks; without this experience you won't be able to make the connections that you need to create great games.

With plenty of game-playing experience under your belt you will be ready to move on to the next stage, designing a game. All games share three common traits. They all have goals, they all have rules and they all give feedback. When implementing a game-based learning approach you will need to think about each of these elements and how they will align to create a compelling learning experience.

Goals

Goals are central to the pedagogical effectiveness of a game. You start out with a problem to be solved and you measure your success in terms of how well you solved it. Aligning the goals of a learning game with your learning requirement is paramount for successful game-based learning.

Whilst games may embody a single overarching goal – save the princess, slay the dragon, win the Champion's League – it is in the breakdown of this goal into simple objectives and steps that most gameplay actually occurs. Ideally, a game adapts the difficulty of these objectives so that a player will be tasked with achieving something that is just slightly beyond their current level of skill within the game. To keep pace with a player's mastery, objectives must increase in difficulty as the game progresses towards its conclusion.

The ultimate aim of this correlation between a player's ability and the challenge of the task at hand is to achieve a state known as "flow". First articulated by psychologist Mihalyi Csikszentmihalyi,[8] flow is said to be the feeling of being completely absorbed in an activity – being "in the zone" (see Figure 10.1). Games that encourage players towards this state tend to completely engage their audience –

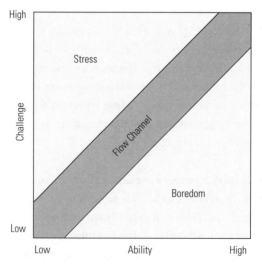

Figure 10.1 *Mihalyi Csikszentmihalyi's flow model*

players can find themselves spending hours on a single experience when in a state of "flow".

Whilst this state sounds like the holy grail of engagement, it comes with a health warning. Literally. Game designers, especially those in South Korea, are under increasing pressure to encourage players to take breaks and step out of the flow zone, lest it be damaging to their health to remain absorbed in a game for too long.

Rules

Whilst games give us the chance to suspend reality and allow us deity-esque powers, they often stop short of giving players complete omnipotence (even Populous, the game where you played a God, had some rules). Players of games operate within constraints that create the mastery imperative – you have to gain in competence to overcome the obstacles. This is where we derive ideas such as "hard fun"; without rules there would be no challenge.

Feedback

Feedback lets players know how they are progressing towards a given goal. The feedback that games give us can help us to evaluate our own self-efficacy for a particular task as well as giving a sense of progress and achievement. Feedback in games can also be used as a means to allow players to understand how and why they might have failed in the pursuit of a given goal. The opportunity to learn from failure is often cited as a defining characteristic of what makes game-based learning effective. Feedback is also used to communicate a win-state; that is, when you have successfully beaten the game, you know about it. Generally speaking, the presence of a win-state is what differentiates games from any other pursuit that involves goals, rules and feedback, like simulations.

Three key elements of a game

Goals, rules and feedback are quite high-level concepts; to actually make a game, we need talk about mechanics, spaces and stories. These elements combine to create the overall game experience, or gameplay. The following brief guide will start you on a path to discovering more about game design theory.

EXAMPLE #1 – THE CRACKER BARREL "JUMP ALL BUT ONE" GAME.

When I was about 10 years old my family went to Disneyland in Florida. I didn't find the Magic Kingdom overly magical, but I did leave Florida with one abiding memory: The Cracker Barrel "Jump all but one" game.

For the unfamiliar, Cracker Barrel is a corporate chain of "old country stores", which adorn American highways; outposts of southern hospitality. The food was memorable for all the wrong reasons (note to self: those three scoops of butter on your pancakes are not vanilla ice cream), but they had a game on each table that you could play whilst you waited to be served.

In the "jump all but one" game, 14 golf tees sit proudly atop a simple wooden triangle block that contains 15 holes. Your task is to "jump" the tees over each other, moving a tee only to a free hole on the other side of the tee to be jumped. Kind of like chequers, when you successfully make a jump you can remove the tee you went over. The challenge is to leave just 1 tee remaining.

The game is hard. It would be easy to suggest after your first go or two that it isn't possible. But right there on the wooden triangle block, seared in with a soldering iron, is the feedback instruction:

> "Leave only one – you're genius
> Leave two and you're purty smart
> Leave three and you're just plain dumb
> Leave four or mor'n you're just plain
> EG-NO-RA-MOOSE"

With my measure of efficacy in one hand and an iron, teelike grip in the other, I played the game for hours until I could beat it consistently. Feedback had let me know the win-state I was going for and I didn't stop until I'd done it. The space wasn't innovative, but it told me everything I needed to know to play the game.

Mechanics

Game mechanics are the constructs that allow players to progress towards their goals; they are the actions that players take in order to progress within the game. Remember, games aren't like real life, they are constrained. Game mechanics represent the exceptions to these constraints; they are what you can do as a player in order to reach the win-state.

Thousands of game mechanics have been established and it tends to be in the juxtaposition of several mechanics that we find a good game experience. For example, in Lara Croft: Tomb Raider, you could "run" and "jump" – two mechanics. But certain puzzles required that you mastered both running and jumping together – the only way to overcome certain obstacles was to master the "running jump", a third mechanic which emerges from combining two other mechanics.

A core mechanic refers to an underlying gameplay property that comes to define the game. For example, Monopoly uses a turn-based core mechanic. This means I can only move when it is my turn. If you played Monopoly in real-time, responding instantly to any other move and throwing dice as fast as you could, the games constraints would fall away and it would cease to be a fun game. Typically, core mechanics are used to define a games genre. You might see terms like "turn-based", "real-time strategy", "first person shooter" and so on.

Spaces

Game mechanics give us the ability to try out new behaviours in a virtual environment and we recognize this in the term "spaces". Proponents of game-based learning will often highlight the ability to experience "safe failure" as one of the key benefits of a game. Better to kill a virtual patient than a real one, after all.

Spaces combine not just the aesthetic of a virtual environment but also the etiquette of the experience. Explicitly declaring a space as a place for playfulness is an absolute requirement when designing game-based learning experiences – we want people to play.

Some spaces seek high fidelity with the real world as a part of the games structure. In these circumstances, replicating real-world rules is often fundamental to the learning outcome. But you don't have to build a 3D world to make a game. You just need to envisage a suitable space in which a game can be played.

Story

The story represents the narrative, the timeline, that you are looking for players to move forward each time they correctly use a games mechanic to meet an objective. Often, mechanics in and of themselves are somewhat tedious after a time (how many vampires can you slay before you've seen them all?) and so the story compels the player to continue on their journey. Whether or not a games designer chooses to create an explicit story to accompany the game, you often find that players create stories for themselves as the game progresses.

Types of games for learning

All sorts of games have been developed for learning. What follows here is far from an exhaustive list, but it should give you an idea for the usual suspects when it comes to the types of games that best suit learning requirements. In choosing a game it is important to keep in mind not only the learning outcomes, but also the commercial constraints within which you are operating and the psychographics of the audience you are reaching out to – will the Women's Institute really want to destroy zombie hoards?

Drill and Practice:

Drill and Practice games are perhaps the simplest examples of consistently successful game-based learning interventions. They ask players to perform a basic task in repetitions often with the aim of reaching rote retention. We can use Drill and Practice games when information is explicit and well defined, for example maths and spelling problems are perhaps the most common uses, but they can be extended to other areas. Of course, this type of game is limited to behaviourist notions of learning and memory; it is unlikely that a player will be compelled to reflect deeply on the meaning of the game.

Many Drill and Practice games are developed in Adobe Flash; increasingly we see these types of games presented as mobile apps. They tend to embody a single mechanic and don't often include much in the way of story or even a well-designed space. In this sense they might not even qualify as a "game", merely an interaction.

EXAMPLE #2 – RECYCLING MADNESS

"It's great, but it shouldn't have a time limit," my client told me. "Throwing rubbish into the right bin is an accurate portrayal of the behaviour we want staff to exhibit, but giving them a 15 second time limit in which to do it isn't realistic. The game would be better if it wasn't limited by time."

Bernard Suits would turn in his grave, if he were dead (which he's not).

I pushed back fairly hard on my client. I explained that we needed to up the stakes if we were to convince players to repeat the exercise and that, for our circumstances, repetition would lead to retention. By presenting a very tight time window (a mechanic) and also suggesting that you could do better (via Feedback), we got players repeating the game, again and again.

Serious games

Serious games are very much like commercial games, with one important difference; they are played for a specific, real-world purpose. We would expect serious games to embody multiple mechanics, a well-defined space and a compelling story. Whilst some serious games are developed for specific company requirements, many reach out to the wider world. America's Army, a First Person Shooter game developed to promote recruitment in the US Army, is often highlighted as the exemplar of this outreach potential.

We can sub-divide serious games into two further categories:

1. Serious games for situated learning
   Realistic serious games allow players to practise situated learning; getting as close to the real thing as possible. These games seek to replicate the precise setting and rules of a real-world experience, for example, a healthcare game being set in a hospital. In high-risk settings, these types of games allow players to explore potential actions in a safe setting. They also have other uses, for example, allowing players to more readily understand their existing workplace behaviour.
2. Serious games for cognitive development
   Not all serious games go for situated learning. Instead, some seek cognitive development above and beyond replicating any particular real-world

situation. This can often take place in an abstracted space, something that is quite deliberately different to reality. Here the mechanics used are more likely to take the form of puzzles or to require players to collaborate in order to progress. A really interesting commercial game to explore in this area is Minecraft, a world-building game. In "creative" mode, the player is free to use the resources and tools to build whatever they want out of cube blocks. Intriguingly some players have taken to building worlds out of this blank canvas – one player going as far as to replicate a 3D globe of the Earth, another player creating a working calculator out of blocks. Perhaps most intriguing of all is the way Minecraft looks – a blocky, pixelated experience straight out of the eighties. It's beautiful only because of players' imagination.

Commercial Off-the-Shelf games (COTS)

One conflict faced by designers of games for workplace learning is the balance between budget and quality. As many of your learners will have been exposed to the quality gameplay that is available in commercial titles, you might often find that your budget doesn't quite do justice to the experience.

So, if you can't beat 'em, join 'em. Plenty of commercial games offer valuable lessons for the workplace, especially those concerned primarily with strategy and decision making. The value of using these games isn't so much in the playing, although that might be a nice aside, it is more in the reflection that you need to facilitate following the encounter.

James Paul Gee, a noted games scholar, talks about the concept of Affinity Spaces as being key to the educational potential of game-based learning. Affinity Spaces refer to the community discussion forums, blogs and collaborative areas that exist outside of games where a community comes together to discuss the game. Affinity Spaces are big deals; did you know for example, that the second largest wiki after Wikipedia is the World of Warcraft wiki?

In the world of COTS games, these spaces become the primary focus for the reflection, integration and resolution of insights gained from the game. They also become a focal point for community outside of the field of play – the digital equivalent of going to the pub after playing a game.

Alternate Reality Games (ARGs)

"The greatest trick the Devil ever pulled was convincing the world he didn't exist."
Roger "Verbal" Kint, The Usual Suspects

Alternate Reality Games (ARGs) are emerging as a fascinating new type of game that can be used for learning experiences. ARGs use the internet as a platform to create a fictional narrative that players can interact with. Typically, ARGs will present themselves as a series of obscure clues to be followed, a treasure hunt of sorts. They often involve players journeying to real-world locations as they are led to them by deciphering clues. Along the way players collaborate with each other to test hypotheses and discuss the "real meaning" behind the story.

One of the central premises of the ARG encounter is the denial that you are actually playing a game – the Puppetmaster (the person controlling the game) will deny that what the players are experiencing is a game. As such, the ARG experience often takes a surreal turn, with players no longer able to distinguish what is real from what is faked.

ARGs take a clever mind to author and a good deal of time to set up but they can actually be developed for very little cost. Websites can be developed quickly and easily (think Wordpress), email addresses and social media accounts are free, even Skype numbers (for setting up "real" phone lines) cost just a few pounds per month.

EXAMPLE #3 – I LOVE BEES

Created somewhat ironically to promote another game, the "I Love Bees" Alternate Reality Game gained a cult following thanks to its compelling storyline. Those who stumbled across an obscure bee-related website were led down the rabbit hole over a series of twists and turns, including the discovery of 200 seemingly randomly paired numbers. The numbers were actually a series of GPS co-ordinates and times that mapped directly to some 200 payphones spread right across the USA. At the precise time specified each phone was rung by the games creators in the hopes of speaking to one or two players who had figured out the clues. Every phone was answered. A compelling storyline really can make your players go "above and beyond" once they have been emotionally brought into a scenario.

Simulations (aka: Not Games)

> *"If they don't get one, I don't get one."*
>
> Ken Mattingly, Apollo 13.

There is an iconic moment in the film Apollo 13 that best describes the nature of simulations. Ken Mattingly, as portrayed by Gary Sinese, is working all hours in the flight simulator to help create a new re-entry procedure for his colleagues stranded in space. Ken is asked if he wants to take a break; "If they don't get one, I don't get one" he replies.

Simulations seek to reproduce the real world with unerring accuracy. Whilst simulations are increasingly realistic in look and feel, it is their fidelity with the rules and conditions that abound in the real world that define them as an experience unto themselves. Simulations have a long history of providing authentic opportunities to practice for the real world and their benefits are beyond doubt (think, for instance, of pilot training).

Where games create artificial barriers for players to overcome, simulations replicate realistic constraints. But simulations lack a "win state". You can do well, but you can never win. As such, simulations shouldn't really be classified as "game-based learning" despite often being thought of as one and the same.

Gamification

Gamification is the concept of applying gamelike feedback to non-game situations. Typically, gamification manifests itself as points, levels and badges which are given out to users based on them performing certain actions in a non-game setting. This approach can be especially useful to engage people in long-term processes where personal progress is difficult to ascertain. We know that short-term rewards are more powerful than perceived long-term benefits; gamification uses this principle to promote short-term engagement with a long-term process.

The term solicits a fair amount of vitriol from both game and learning designers. It is often sold as the "fix" to improving user engagement with learning, but many are suspicious of the technique's longevity and depth, especially when it is applied as an after-thought. It is unlikely that you can make a dull, ineffective piece of training compelling and effective with the use of gamification.

However, gamification can give us a useful tool-set to help shape a change in behaviour. Meaningful metrics are frankly quite sensible in any learning journey. And engagement can be enhanced in certain circumstances. As an example take Foursquare, the geo-location app. Foursquare uses points and badges to get users into the habit of "checking in" at a location. Sometimes these rewards are recognized by the location, for example in certain Starbucks locations you can get a free drink when you earn the "mayor" badge for that branch. Participants can readily be drawn in to competing with each other for these recognition points (there can only be one mayor for instance), thus creating a virtuous circle of participation.

Where gamification is designed into an experience from day one, the overall effect can be profound and most useful. Badgeville, a gamification platform provider, regularly reports increases in audience engagement in the hundreds of percentage points when gamification techniques are employed in the design of a system. The danger is that this engagement is facile in nature, focusing people on rewards not on the underlying behaviour. After time the allure of such rewards can fade and engagement may drop off.

Hints and tips

POST: A really simple acronym to remember when you first start sketching out a project is POST. Originally developed as a part of the "Groundswell" approach to social media marketing, POST is relevant in just about any context. In stands for People, Objectives, Strategy and Technology. Firstly you should evaluate your audience. Who are they, what do they like doing, how long have they got, will they find the topic inherently interesting? Following this you note down the objectives of your project; what would success look like? Armed with these pieces of information you can formulate a Strategy – what sort of game would appeal to both the People and meet the Objectives? Finally, consider Technology; what do you need to make it work?

Consider the wider impact of your game: In most cases games aren't cheap. We've established that you don't need to spend the earth to create a game, but in all likelihood you are still going to be parting with tens of thousands of pounds. But games for learning do have an ace up their sleeve that other options might not be able to carry off – the possibility of wider impact. Not only can games achieve learning outcomes better than some alternatives, but they can also make a splash in terms of marketing, reach and recognition. Truly great games for learning tend to reach beyond the organization's walls – America's Army for instance gathered millions of players. Cost needs to be evaluated in terms of overall impact. It isn't necessarily a problem to create a very expensive game, you just need to be sure of a massive impact. The opposite is equally true. Most games lie along what is known as "the efficient frontier" (see Figure 10.2). This is where cost is in proportion to impact. Great games break the efficient frontier – they punch above their weight. For instance one person with virtually no budget developed "Mindcraft", yet it has reached millions of players. In doing so it set a new benchmark for what might be achieved with little or no budget.

Investigate the next best alternative: You might face a degree of opposition when you come to pitch a game for learning internally. You run the risk of looking like you're just building something because you would like to, not because it makes good business sense. Of course you would never do such a thing! In preparation for such eventualities it is advisable to investigate the "next best alternative" to building a game. What would that look like? What drawbacks would it have?

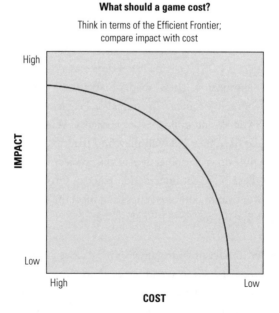

Figure 10.2   *The efficient frontier*

Play it on paper first: Play testing is perhaps the most important part of the game development process – actually getting your game in front of people and getting their feedback. You cannot leave this until the game has been built, it might well be too late by then. You can test out the fundamental mechanics and feedback mechanisms of your game on paper, before you commit anything to code. Do this at the earliest opportunity. Overwhelmingly when I do this I am looking to answer just one question – is it fun? If it's not, re-work the game and try again.

Develop a Game Design Document: In the design of your game you will make many documents. You need to bring the best of these together in a single document that acts as the game's Bible. We call this the Game Design Document. Usually this document will comprise of the story, the characters, the gameplay, some sketches of the aesthetics and finally the codex. The codex is where you document the relationships between variables and work out the maths that lies behind the game. For example, if you decide that certain decisions in a game affect a key performance indicator – safety for instance in a healthcare game – then you will need to document every action that can be taken to affect safety, and by how much. There isn't much science to this in my opinion, it is mostly a case of using your gut feel to begin with and then play testing the numbers to see if it works.

The usual suspects

Game-based learning brings a lot of baggage with it as a phrase. Not many terms in our industry can create quite so much of a stir as the prospect of a game. As such, you might find yourself battling with some familiar jibes when the topic comes up.

Thinking that only certain people play games: We all play games. It's too easy to suggest that certain demographics won't play a game because of their gender, age or seniority. Forget demographics, they tell you nothing about an individual's wants and needs. Instead consider whether this audience will like competition or be turned off by it? Will they enjoy dominating or collaborating?

Thinking that games have to be fun or funny: There's no such thing as enforced fun. Raph Koster suggested that fun comes from achieving mastery of a difficult problem; it's a function of achieving something, not of playing through a witty scenario. The number of games I have played in my life that were genuinely funny I can count on one hand (Portal 2 is hilarious, but they did get a Hollywood star cast to voice the characters). Worry less about fun and more about play. Fun will emerge if the scenarios you set out are challenging and engaging.

Thinking that all games are the same: Game-based learning is a totally inappropriate phrase to be honest. "Games" encompasses such a vast array of interactions that the term on its own loses all meaning. Games in learning are nothing new – it seems very likely that someone in your organization is already using one in some capacity or another.

Thinking that games have to be expensive: Like just about everything else in this life, games range in cost from free to millions of pounds. The only difference is that costs can mount quickly as a game becomes more complex and demanding. In addition, I personally think that vendors of learning technology can sometimes become a little "over-enthusiastic" at the prospect of landing a game-based learning contract. As such, estimates soar. If this is the case, the answer is simple; you need to do more of the work yourself. Which brings us to the next suspect . . .

Thinking that game design is hard: You don't need to be an artist to create a game. Equally you don't need to be a kick-ass programmer. You might need the services of these individuals at some point, but the grunt work, forming the idea and writing the game design document, is achievable by anyone who puts their mind to it.

Thinking that game design is easy: OK, let me re-visit my last statement. It is very, very hard work to design a compelling game. You need to have an excellent eye for detail and a relentless work ethic to create a codex that works for instance. Don't go into it lightly, or with a plate full of other, more important, projects.

Thinking that people won't "game" the system: I have never built a game that people didn't try to cheat in some way shape or form. It just seems to be human nature. On one hand, it's a good sign – people care enough to try and circumvent your mechanics in the search for a better outcome. On the other hand, it can be a very bad sign, for instance when people are circumventing your rules to reach the end more quickly. Placing the focus less on completion and more on "the journey" helps to focus players' attention away from the extrinsic motivation that comes from the pot of gold at the end of the rainbow.

Measuring the wrong thing. When it comes to evaluating the success of game-based learning activities, it is all too easy to measure the wrong metric. Most people concentrate on views, completions and such like. That's great as a pat on the back, but you must remember your original objectives. For a game to have serious impact it needs to fundamentally address a key business objective – get more business, solve real problems, cut bottom-line cost. None of these can be measured with completion statistics.

It's a wrap

"Games need to illuminate aspects of ourselves that we do not understand fully."

Raph Koster[9]

The potential learning benefits of well-designed games are established, but until recently, the commercial proposition for building such interventions had often been lacking. With the rise of new genres in gaming that take advantage of the internet as a platform, we're beginning to see a raft of exciting new possibilities emerge that open the world of games to elearning designers.

Serious Games, ARGs and gamification can all take advantage of the social web to create a new breed of learning game. It is easy (relatively speaking) to create games that tap into the more Neanderthal tendencies of players – to kill, to gain territory, to dominate and destroy. But human instincts go much further than the need to dominate. We are co-operative, creative and thirsty for new knowledge. With game-based learning it seems likely we're on the verge of something great.

Notes

1. Marc Prensky, *Digital Games-Based Learning* (Paragon House Publishers, 2001). He said this a while ago, so his figures might well have moved in recent years.
2. Traci Sitzmann performed a meta-analysis of game-based learning research (which included some games which I'd probably term simulations instead) – "A meta-analytic examination of the Instructional Effectiveness of Computer-based Simulation Games". It represents a solid empirical evidence basis for implementing game-based learning. You might also wish to read a similar study by Sara de Freitas, *Learning in Immersive Worlds: A review of game-based learning*. Simon Egenfeldt-Neilson's 2006 study, *Overview of Research on the Educational Use of Video Games*, is more critical in nature and, as such, probably the best for a balanced view.
3. If you read just one book on game design, make it Jesse Schell's *The Art of Game Design: A book of lenses* (CRC Press, 2008).

4. Tracy Fullerton, *Game Design Workshop: A Playcentric Approach to Creating Innovative Games* (CRC Press, 2008).

5. Jane McGonigal, *Reality is Broken* (Vintage, 2011). Jane's work is at the forefront of using games to save humanity; the I Love Bees ARG is a product of her imagination.

6. Marc LeBlanc, 8 kinds of fun – http://8kindsoffun.com/.

7. Bernard Suits, *The Grasshopper: Games, Life and Utopia* (Broadview Press Limited, 2005),.

8. M. Csikszentmihalyi (Harper & Row, 1990) *Flow: The psychology of optimal experience* is appearing everywhere at the moment. It underpins some key characteristics of what we know about the engagement powers of games.

9. Raph Koster's *A Theory of Fun for Game Design* (Paraglyph Press, 2005) is a seminal book for game designers and educationalists alike. Karl Kapp has written the definitive book on gamification for learning design, see *The Gamification of Learning and Instruction* (John Wiley & Sons, 2012).

11. Learning Management

· Charles Jennings ·

Director of the 70:20:10 Forum and member of the Internet Time Alliance, Australian born **Charles Jennings** is a leading thinker and practitioner in learning and development.

A former academic and business school professor, his 40-year career has taken him to all corners of the earth, and includes roles as Chief Learning Officer at Reuters and Thomson Reuters – the world's largest multimedia information companies – and as director of the UK's national centre for network-based learning.

He has led learning and performance improvement initiatives for multinational corporations, for the UK Government and for the European Commission.

Twitter: @charlesjennings
Website: 702010forum.com

The Really Useful eLearning Instruction Manual. Edited by Rob Hubbard. © 2013 John Wiley & Sons, Ltd.

What's the big idea?

Why do we need systems for "learning management" anyway?

It's now widely agreed that the only person who can "manage" learning is the individual in whose head the learning process is occurring. So the term "learning management" could be considered to be an oxymoron when it isn't referring to neural processes going on inside flesh-and-blood – a little like "*stagnant growth*" or "*your call is very important to us. Your approximate wait time is 15 minutes*". It sounds sensible on first hearing, but doesn't hold up to any thorough analysis.

However it is generally acknowledged that there's a need to manage the *processes* around organizational learning in some, but not all, situations. We need to automate registration and enrolment and manage the allocation of resources – training rooms, trainers and so on – and we need to record the delivery of regulatory and compliance training activity, if for nothing else then to keep our Chief Executives and Board Chairmen out of the courts and prison system!

So "learning *process* management" is what is really being referred to under the umbrella term "learning management". This chapter will look at approaches that have been used and approaches that *can* be used for effective learning process management.

Learning is a continuous process, but we like to break it into discrete events.

Although learning is a continuous process it is often underpinned by a series of learning events in the organizational context. Until relatively recently these learning events were almost exclusively carried out face-to-face in classrooms and workshops. Instructors and students gathered together at set times and set places to work through a programme or curriculum of study and carry out activities that usually led to some form of assessment, certification or accreditation.

Process management and record keeping are two very important components of this type of structured learning, as they are of the electronic equivalent – course-based elearning.

It's not important that this process management used to be called "training administration" and was usually carried out through manual record keeping. There's still a need for training process management in the twenty-first century organization, however there is not so much need for it as there used to be.

The pendulum has swung towards a greater need to "manage" and support learning in totally new and different ways as work changes and almost everything speeds up. We have passed a point where simply updating old processes is good enough to meet current needs. We need to rethink our approaches from ground up.

In other words, "learning management" is taking on entirely new meanings.

Learning management systems

In order to make the best decisions today and in the future, it's important to understand a little about the origins of learning management technology and the developments over the past half-century. Although knowing "what got us here won't necessarily get us where we need to be" (thanks to Marshall Goldsmith), it does help us understand the background thinking and constraints. It also helps us make informed decisions in terms of:

1. The strategic approach we take to learning management
2. What needs to be "managed"
3. What needs to be reported
4. What "fit for purpose" means in terms of tools and technologies
5. The prioritization of learning management processes.

Learning management systems: some background

Learning Management Systems (LMS) emerged in their current form from a desire to automate manual process management and record-keeping systems. There was a requirement for efficiency to match the efficiencies that were being made elsewhere across organizations with financial and other people management systems (now called HRMSs). If technology could replace manual record keeping then this was seen as a "good thing" and something that should be aspired to.

The LMS world has its genesis in the "integrated learning systems" in the 1960s. The term "LMS" was originally used to describe the management module of the PLATO Computer Assisted Instruction system which was developed at the University of Illinois in 1960. PLATO emerged from earlier work in response to the challenge of the post-World War II veteran influx into education and training when ideas about automation and factory production were at their peak.

PLATO was built to deal with large-scale, relatively homogeneous learning demands where speed of throughput was essential and many of the processes supporting training were standardized and replicable. PLATO was in use in universities and schools for many years. The system deployed the first touch screen technology in the 1970s and the technology evolved until the last PLATO system was shut down in 2006.

Most of today's learning management systems are still recognizable as children of PLATO – built primarily as delivery and management tools for "Automated Teaching Operations" (the "ATO" part of PLATO).

Figure 11.1 shows learning with a PLATO terminal in the 1970s – note the touch-screen technology

Today's learning management systems

Today's learning management systems have evolved into highly complex (often over-complex) tools. With the rapid growth of course-based elearning over the past 15 years LMS tools have adapted and adopted additional functionality to meet the need for launching and tracking use. Other new requirements have emerged, including linking the output of LMS tools with HR systems, support for competency maps and curricula-building tools. There has also been focus on integrating, or linking to, learning content management (LCMS) functionality and so on.

At the same time, LMS vendors have managed to position their products at the centre of organizational learning and development. Many organizations devoted significant budgets and resources to purchasing and maintaining learning management

Figure 11.1 *Learning with a PLATO terminal in the 1970s*
© Courtesy of the University of Illinois Archives, Photographic Subject File, RS 39/2/20

systems. In the decade following the emergence of content-centric elearning delivered over intranets and the internet (1999–2009) the LMS became the manifestation of organizational learning provision for many. The LMS and the organization's learning offerings were one-and-the-same.

Thankfully, we are moving beyond that situation. The new world of workplace and social learning is opening up both new challenges and new opportunities for learning management.

When do you need a learning management system?

The LMS is certainly not dead, but it is worthwhile reviewing the type of situations where one is necessary.

Process automation

Almost every organization needs a set of automated tools to manage its standardized training processes. Whether structured event-based learning in classrooms, off-site programmes for managers, workshops, or elearning courses or modules.

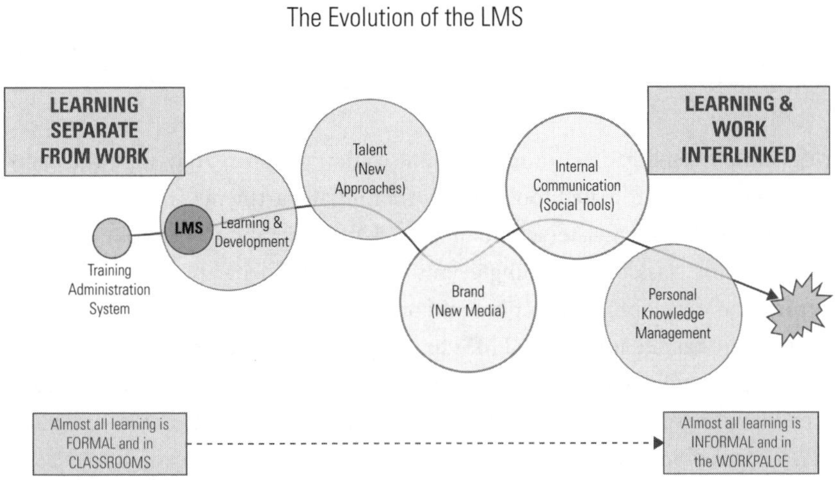

The Evolution of the LMS

Figure 11.2   *The evolution of the LMS in organizations*

Regulatory and compliance training

Automated registration and distribution of content, provisioning, and attendance and attainment recording are vital parts of every form of regulatory and compliance training programme. Failure to accurately record progress and completion of mandatory training can result in fines and worse for senior executives. However as the management of learning becomes increasingly complex and the need for "real-time learning" becomes a greater imperative we need to ask – and answer – some questions about the applicability of 1960 industrial models to the much more flexible and agile world of the twenty-first century.

Figure 11.2 shows the path learning management systems have travelled from their origin as automated training administration tools.

LMS evolution is well underway. As integrated talent approaches are embedded and it becomes apparent that social media and social tools are weaving strands through marketing and corporate communications departments, it is clear that LMS evolution is not only necessary, but inevitable. Another factor playing an important role is the merging of learning and work and the realization by HR and learning and development departments that they need to address the difficult issue of integrating informal, social and workplace learning into their strategic and operational plans.

As we travel along this path, the role of personalized learning will also expand and the evolution of learning infrastructure will need to adapt to support that trend as well.

LMSs initially emerged as training administration systems. They were the central (and often only) automated tool used by training departments. Their purpose was to record enrolment, register attendance, track progress and record completion and test results for classroom training events. As training departments morphed into learning and development functions and organizations, the training administration systems were carried forward as LMSs to complete similar tasks, but with the added complexity brought about by the emergence of elearning and an increased focus on embedding learning into the HR operating rhythm of job role curricular and annual development objectives.

The past five years have placed even more strain on the demands of LMS technology.

Give me the details

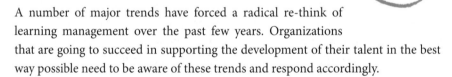

Rethinking learning management

A number of major trends have forced a radical re-think of learning management over the past few years. Organizations that are going to succeed in supporting the development of their talent in the best way possible need to be aware of these trends and respond accordingly.

Five of the most significant trends are discussed below:

1. The changing nature of course-based elearning
2. The changing nature of work
3. The rise of the extended enterprise
4. The rise and rise of social and workplace learning
5. The challenges of learning management and HR integration.

Trend 1: Changing nature of course-based elearning

The emergence of online elearning into the mainstream in the late 1990s was the first major departure from a two-thousand-year continuum of the classroom being the core of learning. Although computer-based training (CBT) had been used by many organizations for the previous decade the move from stand-alone and locally-networked systems to online provision, enabled by Tim Berners-Lee and Robert Cailliau's development of the World Wide Web and the lowering cost of computing power, enabled a major disruption in the world of classroom-based training.

Organizations came to terms with the idea that people could complete modules and courses of formal training at any time and from virtually anywhere through networks. elearning grew rapidly, and is continuing to do so.

Initially, elearning mimicked traditional classroom-based learning by being content-centric and taking a relatively long time to complete. Modules lasting 60 or 90 minutes were common, and these were sometimes aggregated into elearning courses of several hours. Today elearning modules have tended to become shorter and more interactive (although "electronic page-turners" are sometimes still being produced).

The past ten years have also seen the rise of "blended" approaches where elearning is integrated with face-to-face classroom and workshop activities. "Blending" has moved from the initial "top-and-tail" model – where pre-work and post-course assessments were delivered as elearning modules wrapped around traditional classroom teaching – to more integrated designs where elearning is used for content delivery and face-to-face classroom sessions are used for activity-based learning that can be best carried out with a group of people together in one place at one time. This is sometimes referred to as a "flipped classroom" approach.

The rise of the "flipped classroom" and "flipped teaching" movements[1] demonstrates a better application of elearning in all its forms and its integration with classroom learning. Managing learning in the "flipped" world poses new challenges.

Trend 2: Changing nature of work

The social context of work is changing, and the tools and technologies being used to carry out work are also rapidly evolving. The percentage of practical transactional work such as factory work, manual jobs and other work done with hands rather than brain, especially in the developed economies, is contracting while work requiring decisions and management of tacit knowledge is expanding. Some time ago McKinsey and Co. reported[2] that "70 percent of all US jobs created since 1998 required judgment and experience". By 2005 these *tacit* jobs made up 41% of the labour market in the United States. The percentage of these jobs is increasing year-on-year.

The implications that these changes bring for managing, supporting and encouraging learning and building workforce capability are clear. Speed to competence and innovation will be key determining factors in organizational success. Learning has a crucial part to play, but only if a culture of continuous learning is supported and encouraged. Organizations need to build learning strategies that are responsive to rapid change and their approaches to facilitating and managing learning will play an important part.

The increasing need for agility in the workplace will require increased agility in the approaches taken in learning and development to support workers. If we fail to grasp this fact learning and development departments will become backwaters.

As learning and work become inseparable, getting our approaches for supporting and "managing" learning right will become critical.

Trend 3: The rise of the extended enterprise

There is no doubt that huge changes are afoot in the workplace. Hierarchies are flattening, organizational boundaries are softening and extending and even the traditional concepts of a "job" and a "role" are being questioned as work becomes more focused on bringing the right expertise together at the right time to solve specific problems and challenges.

Josh Bersin, CEO of Bersin by Deloitte, calls this world "the borderless workplace" – an ecosystem where workers communicate continually and seamlessly across time and distance with co-workers both inside and outside their own organization. Bersin's research leads him to the view that high-performing organizations are re-aligning from role-based work to task-based work. Bersin says:[3]

> *"This change, coupled with the globalization of our markets, has redefined what a 'job' really is."*

These changes have significant implications for our approach to learning management. If the organization of work is moving more towards task focus it will mean that workers won't necessarily have a single line manager, nor will role-based learning (a fundamental element of many current LMSs) continue to be relevant. These changes also mean that the workplace will become even more dynamic, with teams forming, doing their work, and then disbanding as workers move onto new projects and business challenges. Managing learning in this environment will look very different from managing learning in the stable, structured world from which the LMS toolset emerged.

Trend 4: The rise and rise of social and workplace learning

The twin trends of increased social media use and increased focus on learning in the workplace have already had a profound impact on organizational learning and will, without doubt, continue to do so.

These two general trends bring with them significant challenges for existing approaches to learning management. Fundamental to these challenges is the fact that most social learning and most workplace learning can't be "managed" in the traditional sense. Environments can be created to support social and workplace learning but "management" of processes is out of the hands of both the organization and the learning and development department.

This raises the obvious question. "If we can't manage this type of learning, what can we do?" The answer is that there is quite a lot that can be done, but it requires new thinking about when "learning management" is appropriate and when it is best to simply let employees manage their own learning and development in their own preferred ways.

We are already seeing top young talent eschewing opportunities to join organizations where access to the systems and tools they prefer to use to support them at work – social networks such as Facebook and Twitter and technologies such as smartphones and tablets – are banned and where learning systems are not as accessible or appealing to use.

In December 2011 the Australian telecom company Optus released a study on the future of the workplace based on interviews with IT and HR executives. This group predicts that allowing employees to have access to social media will become increasingly important for productivity, staff retention and satisfaction within the next five years.

A survey in the UK[4] also released in late 2011 revealed that half of employees between 16 and 24 years refuse to work for an employer that bans social media at work. Almost 60% of those polled are convinced that having access to social networking sites would increase their effectiveness in the workplace. This study reported:

> "Employers who impose strict policies against the use of social networking tools designed for business are at risk of alienating 'Generation Facebook' from joining their organization."

There are clear implications for learning management emerging from these trends.

The first implication is that organizations need to develop clear strategies on both the approaches and technologies they will use to support and encourage social and workplace learning.

The second implication is that organizations also need to decide to what extent their existing learning management infrastructure should support social and workplace learning and where they need to adopt other tools and approaches.

One school of thought is that existing LMS infrastructure should be extended to incorporate social and workplace learning tools. Another is that existing LMS infrastructure should be used for what it was designed to do – manage formal learning processes such as enrolling employees for classroom training courses and programmes, and launching and tracking elearning modules – and nothing more.

Claire Schooley, a senior analyst at Forrester, falls into the former camp. Schooley identifies a new role for LMS, saying:

> "it needs to integrate informal learning tools (including social); provide Amazon-type content evaluation and rating; allow flexibility to take courses offline and on mobile devices, and provide robust tagged content search so learners can instantly find a piece of content or document."

Others, such as Jay Cross, a respected informal and workplace learning expert, fall into the latter camp. Cross sees the use of the traditional LMS differently. He says:

> "LMS have their place: opening up and tracking performance of formal and compliance training. However, the more mature the worker, the less

dependence on the LMS and the greater the need for social network solutions. Old pros don't take classes. If all you offer is via an LMS, you are failing to support the biggest money-makers in your organization. Duh!"

Trend 5: HR integration: the implications for learning management

Recently there has been a significant push for the integration of learning management with other HR and business processes.

Not only have the last 15 years seen the emergence of enterprise-wide performance management systems, talent management systems and other HR process tools and HRMSs, but also wider strategic and operational workforce planning environments linking the "human resources" needed to deliver wider organizational goals. Learning management systems have been incorporated into these ecosystems to some extent.

Performance management and learning management: the links

Performance management, like learning management, has its origins in the middle of the last century. Performance management processes were primarily developed for managers to justify (or not) the salary being paid to their workers in terms of individual worker productivity. As with learning management, performance management systems over the years have become more sophisticated and extensive – encompassing various types of feedback such as 360-degree and competency-based processes. In addition, new technical systems have emerged to support talent management processes.

On the surface, the integration of performance management, talent management, and learning management offers quite a compelling argument. If HR departments have a single platform from which to support a range of linked HR processes, there is the potential to reduce effort and costs through integration and synergies, and overall technology costs can be brought down by purchase of an integrated solution.

However, as will be explained later in this chapter, this integration comes with significant costs: those of agility and flexibility. These are two very important factors in organizational success in the twenty-first century.

So how do I do it?

What needs tracking in an LMS?

Organizations need to track learning processes for a number of reasons:

- For compliance:
    Many regulatory and compliance requirements are underpinned by rigorous tracking and recording structures. Organizations need to comply with these.
- For assessment of progress:
    Most organizations need (or want) to track the extent and rates of progress that their employees (and, sometimes, others in their value chains) achieve through learning content.
- For certification/accreditation:
    Many organizations need to track completion data for employees and their wider communities for certification and accreditation purposes.

What learning analytics do we need?

Learning management and learning analytics[5] are inextricably linked. Learning has always been driven or supported by analytics of one type or another, although not necessarily with the name learning analytics. One of the main *raisons d'être* for learning measurement has been to justify budget allocation for employee training and development, and one of the main *raisons d'être* for LMS has been to provide the ability of training and development departments to track and measure learning.

Learning measurement, until recently, has fallen into two basic categories:

1. The measurement of individual learning activity.
2. The measurement of individual learning results.

The early training administration and learning management systems measured learning activity by recording attendance in classrooms or access to elearning courses or modules. They also almost invariably measured learning results through recording scores in post-class or post-elearning course assessment tests and certification.

With the increasing focus on workplace and informal learning, not only has the landscape of learning management become much more complex and nuanced, but that of learning analytics (which is closely linked) is also changing.

In addition, our understanding of "real" learning has improved and the implications on measuring learning are profound. Eric Kandel, Nobel Laureate for his work on learning and memory, describes "learning" as follows:

> "'Learning' is the ability to acquire new ideas from experience and retain them as memories."

Kandel's view of learning is firmly rooted in a clear distinction between short-term memory retention (which isn't considered "real" learning) and longer-term retention that changes behaviour and response in particular situations. Measuring the latter must be carried out in the context of applying knowledge and learned behaviours.

There is no doubt we need to rethink what needs measuring and which measurement and analytics will add real value.

The activity measurement tools that are built into virtually all existing LMS platforms have tended to deflect from measuring the things that really matter. Class attendance, elearning module completion and immediate post-module/course results may help the training and development department sleep at night, but they tell the organization nothing about the amount and nature of learning and development that is going on.

How can we change the focus of learning results measurement?

The current focus of learning measurement is moving from an emphasis on activity measurement to results measurement. It is no longer seen as sufficient to simply gather and report data about the amount of time employees spend in classes and the number of courses provided each year. In the past the first step was to measure an individual's completion and success in post-class tests and assessments. Now a further shift is occurring with greater focus being applied to measuring performance results rather than learning results. No longer is it considered sufficient to collect and report the output of post-course assessments and certifications. This is being replaced by focus on the measurement of performance change. There is also a discernible trend from measuring individual results to measuring results in the context of teams and entire organizational performance.

These trends place a lens on the usefulness of the current crop of learning management systems and on their ability to support the measurement of individual and team workplace learning and performance improvement.

The steering committee of the Learning Analytics 2011 Conference[6] has defined learning analytics as:

> "the measurement, collection, analysis and reporting of data about learners and their contexts, for purposes of understanding and optimizing learning and the environments in which it occurs."

Although focused on individual "learners", this view adds yet another perspective – that of the context in which any newly learned skills and capabilities are to be learned and then used. All learning is contextual – without context we learn very little indeed. The challenge of gathering useful learning analytics is that workers find themselves both learning and working in multiple contexts as part of their daily working experience.

Gathering useful learning analytics and measuring the impact of learning is thus a complex business and often not one that can be completely devolved to electronic systems. Learning analytics are often so nuanced that "real" people are needed to make judgements on the meaning of data and to ask the right question at the right time to determine the quality of the learning that has occurred.

Some attempts are being taken to measure "real" learning in terms of changed behaviours and performance. Specialist learning assessment companies have recently focused on the development of tools and approaches for **observational assessment**.

Observational assessments are usually carried out in the workplace. They involve an observer (often a manager, colleague or learning specialist) watching a subject perform a certain task or follow a particular process. The observer answers questions about the subject's activities and rates his or her performance according to pre-determined criteria. The observer then enters the results in an assessment management system. This data is saved, scored and used for reporting of performance gains.

Observational assessment and other workplace measurement approaches will inevitably become more widespread as workplace learning is increasingly adopted. This raises questions for LMS vendors in terms of how, or whether, they should adapt their systems to accommodate support of learning in context and support of the measurement of learning in context.

A key lesson from observational assessment, as well as new thinking on assessment generally, is that the best metrics to use are business metrics, not learning metrics. This requires a major change in thinking for LMS vendors and specialist assessment tool companies as it requires new ways to capture and analyse performance and impact data and to make causal links back to learning and development activities and processes.

The change in emphasis and focus to business metric-driven measurement also requires changes in approach for learning and development professionals. It means that they need to be skilled in performance analysis and in understanding business drivers if they are to select and measure the right factors. They also need good analytic skills to link these causally in some way back to learning interventions.

How can we manage learning across the value chain?

Currently most organizations build their learning infrastructure around the needs of their "established" employees. These are the people who are directly employed on continuing contracts. In other words, people in established roles in their organization which we would call "permanent employees" to distinguish them from contractors, consultants and other workers not on the organization's payroll.

On the surface it makes strategic sense, therefore, to integrate learning management infrastructure with other HR management systems and tools (HRMSs).

This integration allows co-ordination with other HR processes, particularly performance and talent management, with the provision of learning and development services. Almost every organization employs HR processes that include annual or twice-yearly performance reviews which are integrated with, or linked to, development discussions and planning. The output is usually a development plan. In the past, these plans were usually a list of classroom courses and workshops to be attended during the next year. In the past ten years or so they have become more "blended" to include elearning courses and modules and more non-curricular development activities – job shadows, coaching and mentoring activities, job swaps and other experiential development opportunities.

However there is a major challenge to the effectiveness of this approach. Organizations are increasingly looking to work more closely with their value chains. They expect to intermingle many of their processes with their supply chain, their distributors and resellers and, more recently, with their customers.

This increase of value chain integration runs at odds with the tight internal coupling of learning management systems and processes with other HR processes. If learning management is serving people across the value chain then many will not be employees and any HR integration will serve no purpose.

If we are to manage learning processes and provide learning opportunities across the value chain we need to think carefully before we couple any learning management system to other organizational systems.

What's beyond the traditional LMS?

There are a number of solutions emerging that offer alternatives to the traditional LMS route for supporting and managing learning.

The open source option

Moodle has led the way in the open source LMS world. Although positioned as a "standard" LMS, Moodle offers a level of flexibility that is not available from other major bespoke LMS vendors.

Moodle was originally conceived and developed by Martin Dougiamas, but is now maintained and further developed by specialists and amateurs around the world. As such, it is an **open source** tool.

Dougiamas is an Australian who spent his childhood in the desert of Western Australia and was schooled through technology (radio and light aircraft delivered learning content to his remote desert settlement). He understood the need for simplicity and openness in terms of learning technology.

Although the initial uptake of Moodle was in universities and other academic organizations (the UK Open University deployed Moodle in 2005 and is one of the largest users with more than 700,000 registrations in its Moodle database) some extremely large commercial organizations have adopted this Open Source LMS technology. Companies such as Tesco, the international grocery and home goods retailer, and Michelin China, the world's largest tyre manufacturer, provide excellent examples of companies using Moodle for large-scale elearning deployment.

In December 2011 Tesco deployed a new learning portal driven by the Totara LMS from Kineo. Totara is based on Moodle. With Totara in place Tesco was able to deliver a rollout of elearning to its 400,000 employees. In addition to reducing costs significantly, this elearning ecosystem has delivered on the promise of ease of use, sophisticated programme management and an engaging learner experience.

There is clearly no doubt that Moodle, and other open source LMS solutions, will continue to increase market share. An analogy of Moodle's potential could be drawn with Linux, the open source operating system. In the early days of Linux many organizations had reservations about its reliability, stability and security. Today Linux powers at least one-third of all webservers and a huge range of devices from smartphones to high-end, high-security Government and financial industry servers. The US Department of Defence is the "single biggest install base for Red Hat Linux"[7] in the world.

It may be that in the future, learning which needs to be "managed" in organizations will be managed by open source technology. Tools such as the 'Experience API' may also have a role.

Social learning in a managed learning world

Another type of tool for managing learning is emerging. These are the social learning platforms.

Some social learning platforms are pure social media tools that have simply been adapted for use in learning and development. Many organizations are using wikis and blogs powered by standard internet engines for learning and development purposes.

The CIA's Intellipedia is a well-known example of the adaption of standard wiki technology for collaborative data-sharing and learning by the US Intelligence Community. Intellipedia consists of three wikis that allow the collaborative capturing and sharing of up-to-date knowledge across the enterprise. The platform has been hugely successful as a learning and content management tool.

Other organizations have successfully deployed social learning management tools.

- NASA's Spacebook: an internal onboarding and expert networking site for employees. Spacebook supports forums, groups and updates. It has allowed NASA to reduce onboarding training effort.
- Pfizer's Pfizerpedia: This platform contains how-to videos and more than 10,000 articles and blogs across different divisions. Pfizer's Regulatory Affairs Group has embraced it as a suitable platform to manage and deliver training materials.

The new breed of social learning management platforms

There are other social learning management platforms that have been built specifically for use in supporting social and other forms of learning.

An early example was British Telecom's Dare2Share system. Peter Butler, the chief learning officer at British Telecom, found through a staff survey that:

> "78% of our staff learn more from each other than they ever do from a formal learning environment."

As a result, Butler oversaw the building of the Dare2Share platform. This provided BT employees with the ability to learn from each other by rapidly capturing and spreading learning throughout the organization in the form of podcasts, discussion threads, blogs, RSS feeds and other traditional knowledge assets (documents, courses and portals).

FUSE, from British company Fusion Universal, is a second-generation social learning platform. FUSE provides a good example of a video-centric social platform. It incorporates the concepts from popular social media platforms such as YouTube, Facebook, Twitter and LinkedIn and provides an environment for support and management of formal and social learning at the point of need via any computer or mobile device.

These social learning management systems are just a taste of what is to come over the next few years.

Hints and tips

1. Focus most of your effort on supporting learning, not trying to manage it.

    Although managing learning is important in specific circumstances (for regulatory and compliance purposes, for example), it is important that learning management and measurement doesn't become a cottage industry and consume too many resources. The prime focus needs to be on high-value activities such as designing the most effective approaches to support learning as part of the daily workflow. Sometimes it is appropriate that learning is managed. Much of the time it isn't.

2. Think carefully about which learning activities need to be measured.

    The old adage "what gets measured matters" is not always true. Many things that are not measured, and cannot be measured, matter a great deal and many things that are easily measurable don't matter. Equally, many aspects of employee learning and performance development are very difficult or impossible to measure simply or only through technology.

3. Think of the "learning management" beyond LMS technology.

    Most individual learning management is out of the hands of both the learning and development department and LMS technology. By far the greater majority of learning process, and all the learning output, is managed by individual employees together with their manager. We alone can really manage our own learning – although learning and development professionals and LMS technology sometimes have a role in helping to manage parts of the learning process – but if we define "learning" as changes in behaviour that lead to better performance, neither can control learning itself. LMS technology can help, but there are parts that learning management technology can't reach.

4. Avoid falling behind the curve.

The world of learning is changing rapidly. Not just with all the new technologies and devices, but with new ideas and new approaches too. It is important that learning and development professionals continually explore the opportunities offered by new approaches and tools, and carry out critical reviews and pilots. Learning technology is an important area for innovation as it offers potential to support learning at "the speed of change".

The usual suspects

1. Don't be under the illusion that all learning can, or needs to, be managed.

Most learning simply can't be managed. It happens out of sight of the training and development department in the workplace. This doesn't mean it is any less important or valuable. In fact it is often more valuable than away-from-workplace learning. We need to accept this fact and focus on providing rich learning environments that support continuous learning.

2. Don't be under the illusion that all learning needs to be measured.

Effective measurement is sometimes critical. At other times measurement is neither appropriate nor worthwhile. There is often great pressure for learning and development to demonstrate results and this is sometimes expressed in the "measurement argument" – "what gets measured matters". Most organizations measure the value of just a few essential outputs that provide them with relevant and important data to inform action. It is important that learning measurement adopts this approach.

3. Don't let LMS technology restrict your thinking and action.

LMS technology is a useful addition for supporting learning, especially where structured courses and programmes are involved. An LMS is also extremely useful where compliance and mandatory training is necessary. Most LMSs will support the essential processes such as tracking, recording and reporting completion and assessment results. A good LMS will do this much more efficiently than can be done manually. However, more nuanced types of learning – learning within the workflow, learning through participation in discussion and activities with colleagues, and other forms of experiential learning – will often fall outside the ability of LMS technology to manage or track. Don't let that be a reason for ignoring those important aspects of organizational learning and development activity.

4. **Don't be afraid to dispense with your LMS.**

   In some cases it is best to totally dispense with the traditional idea of "learning management" and acknowledge that "learning facilitation" and "learning support" are approaches that achieve better results. Innovative hi-tech companies especially have come to this conclusion. Any system or process that slows or restricts the speed of change and generation of new ways of working is dispensed with. What matters is the ability to stay ahead of "the pack". At least one leading global technology company has moved its onboarding sales training from formal to mobile and social. Where the learning activities of new hires were previously tracked and measured they are now measured by their work performance alone. The company has found this has shortened speed to competence and improved overall performance.

It's a wrap

There are many systems that can be used for managing and supporting learning. However a fine balance is needed to ensure that learning management systems don't become a constraint.

It is important to remember that only a small percentage of all the learning that is occurring within an organization and through interaction of employees with other parties – suppliers, distributors, customers and clients, external professional groups and networks – can, or should, be "managed" in any way. Therefore it is vital that "learning management" does not become the centre of the universe for training and development departments.

A good model to use to determine whether learning can and should be managed is contained in Figure 11.3. It shows that only some 10% or so of learning that occurs is structured, directed and can be managed. The other 90% or so can be supported, encouraged, or simply occurs without any input from learning professionals.

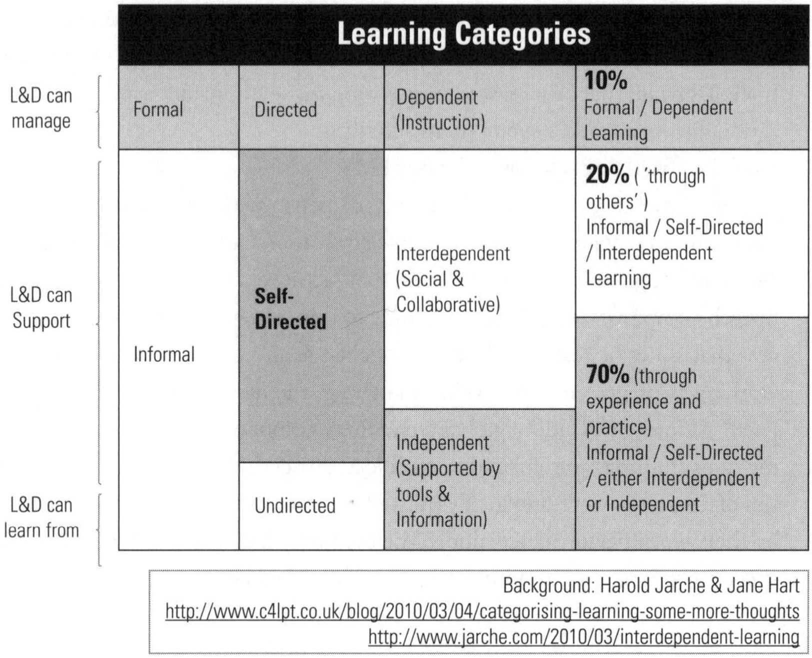

	Learning Categories			
L&D can manage	Formal	Directed	Dependent (Instruction)	**10%** Formal / Dependent Learning
L&D can Support	Informal	**Self-Directed**	Interdependent (Social & Collaborative)	**20%** ('through others') Informal / Self-Directed / Interdependent Learning
				70% (through experience and practice) Informal / Self-Directed / either Interdependent or Independent
L&D can learn from		Undirected	Independent (Supported by tools & Information)	

Background: Harold Jarche & Jane Hart
http://www.c4lpt.co.uk/blog/2010/03/04/categorising-learning-some-more-thoughts
http://www.jarche.com/2010/03/interdependent-learning

Figure 11.3   *Learning categories*

Notes

1. http://en.wikipedia.org/wiki/Flip_teaching.
2. McKinsey Quarterly Q4 2005.
3. http://www.forbes.com/sites/joshbersin/2012/01/31/the-end-of-a-job-as-we-know-it/2/.
4. Study by Hyphen – a UK recruitment process outsourcing company www.hyphen.com.
5. Learning analytics is the measurement, collection, analysis and reporting of data about learners and their contexts for purposes of understanding and optimizing learning and the environments in which it occurs.
6. Learning and Knowledge Analytics. George Siemens, 14 April 2011 http://www.learninganalytics.net/?p=126.
7. Linux.com http://archive09.linux.com/feed/61302.

Index

Index compiled by Mike Solomons